SERVING AS A BOARD MEMBER?

Protecting Yourself from Legal Liability
While Serving Charities

Serving
as a
Board Member?

Dick L. Kranendonk

Essence

P U B L I C A T I O N S

Belleville, Ontario, Canada

SERVING AS A BOARD MEMBER?

ISBN: 1-896400-87-6

Essence Publishing is a Christian Book Publisher dedicated to furthering the work of Christ through the written word. For more information, contact: 44 Moira Street West, Belleville, Ontario, Canada K8P 1S3. Phone: 1-800-238-6376 • Fax: (613) 962-3055. Email: info@essence.on.ca Internet: www.essence.on.ca

Printed in Canada
by

Essence
PUBLISHING

To my family

Hendrika,
Henry, Robert, Reny and Paul

Table of Contents

    The "gift"
    Redesignating a prior gift
    Designated bequests
    Endowment funds
    Are board members trustees?
    Responsibilities if board members are trustees
    Fundraising inducements
    Deputized fundraising
    Private vs. public benevolence
    Deputized fundraising and public benevolence
    Designation and private benevolence
    Detached, disinterested generosity
    Conclusion on gift issues
    Questions for consideration

Delegating powers of the board
Making sure that board policies and decisions are
    implemented properly
Rules of order
The Board acting through committees
The audit committee
Members of the audit committee
Requirement to appoint an executive committee and an
    audit committee
Other committees
Legal role and task of each board member
Board members as trustees of a charitable organization
Board members as agents of the charitable organization
Questions for consideration

The duty of honesty
The duty of loyalty
The duty of care
The duty of diligence
The duty of skill
The duty of prudence
Contracting with other board members or bodies
Attending meetings
Agreement with actions of the board
The right to participate and to be informed
Relying on other board members
Relying on officers
Relying on written reports
Relying on outside experts
Honorary, alternate, and *ex-officio* members
Doing nothing
Seeing no evil
Conflict of interest

Permanent contract or continuing appointment
Termination of employment
Confidentiality
Organizational charts
Advisors to the CEO
Staff attendance at board meetings
Staff speaking at board meetings
Absence of the CEO
Questions for consideration

.

Preface and Acknowledgements

The purpose of this book is to provide charity board members with the information they need about their powers, duties and responsibilities. There is no intent to give legal or other professional advice to the reader. This book should be viewed, solely, as an educational tool designed to help board members to ask the right questions of themselves, the charity's administrators and their professional advisors.

It is my intent to present the material in this book so that it will communicate to the average reader who has been elected or appointed to the governing board of a charity. For this reason, I will avoid technical language wherever possible. In addition, I will not make use of footnotes or endnotes.

The material presented in this book is an accumulation of what I have learned about charities, their purposes, activities and challenges, over the past number of decades. During that time, I have served on the governing boards of a variety of charitable organizations – both incorporated and unincorporated. I have also had extensive experience in the administration of charities as an executive officer of a number of them. I have served for more that ten years as Vice-President (Administration and Finance) of Redeemer College, Ancaster, Ontario, a university college. I am currently the Director, Trust Services at the

Canadian Council of Christian Charities – an umbrella service organization with more than eleven-hundred certified and associate member charities in Canada. Some of these certified and associate members, themselves, represent hundreds of charities. Experience gained in conducting governance and administration audits for a number of CCCC certified charities also helped to focus my attention on the major issues which are important to charities and their board members.

Finally, some of the material presented in this book is based on personal research and experiences during my years of service on Revenue Canada's Charities Consultative Committee.

From the above, it is obvious that my experience in the charitable sector has been in Canada. However, in writing this book, I have attempted to address some of the principles underlying the issues faced by board members of charities. These principles of common law apply both to the United States and Canada. The legal system of both countries is based on British common law. Since there is very little codified law in the area of the organization and administration of charities, and since trust law lies at the base of much of what a charity is and does, trust law is our greatest source of information.

Although this book is written for members of governing boards of all charities in the United States of America and Canada, the reader should be aware that I have gained nearly all of my charity experience in the religious charitable sector. It is difficult to obtain precise information on the percentage of charities which are religiously based: However, it is safe to say, based on information available from the taxation authorities in both countries, that the majority of charities are religious charities, including places of worship.

Since the majority of charities in the United States of America and Canada are churches and related religious organizations, governments are beginning to focus more attention on the religious charitable sector. Therefore, it would be prudent for ministers, elders, deacons or stewards, who form the governing boards and administration of a church, to become familiar with the legal landscape within which churches and para-church organizations operate.

The information in this book was a result of my interaction with many organizations and people. Therefore, it is difficult to acknowledge all those who influenced me. At the risk of neglecting to mention some individuals, I want to identify those who had a significant impact on my thinking. The persons who I wish to single out are Frank Luellau, Executive Director, and Ronald Knechtel, Senior Advisor of the Canadian Council of Christian Charities. I have had many hours of fruitful discussions with them about much of the subject matter in this book. In addition, the substance of their respective writings and public presentations invariable have found their way into the present text. That is not to say that they are in any way responsible for the contents. The responsibilities for the contents of this book are mine exclusively.

I should also acknowledge that I previously published a significant amount of the material in this book in a publication titled *Governance and Management Handbook of Canadian Registered Charities*, 1995, Canadian Council of Christian Charities, 28 Arthur Street South, Elmira, Ontario N3B 2M5. However, that publication focussed primarily on the Ontario legal landscape in a more technical way. I wish to express my appreciation to CCCC for allowing me to make use of my earlier work.

It is my hope that this book will serve in some small way to help educate the board members of charities.' If that is the case, my objective will have been met and the charitable sector and the public in general will have been served.

Dick L. Kranendonk, Ed.D.
Hamilton, Ontario, Canada
Email: dkran@hotmail.com

Introduction

John once told me how he had been elected to the board of a charity involved in international relief and development work. I asked him how his election had come about. He thought it was because he had been a significant donor to the organization for some time, and that he had gained significant respect in his own community.

John had been very successful in his construction business. He had built a number of schools, a hospital and numerous office and commercial buildings. As a result, he had earned a good living, owned a valuable construction company, and had gained the respect of many of the influential members of his community.

John viewed his election to the board of directors of the relief and development agency as a recognition of his position in the local community and as a way of volunteering. In being asked to serve on this board, John believed that he was being honoured by the organization.

I congratulated him with his election to the board of the relief and development organization. I told him that I was glad that he wanted to volunteer by serving as a board member. But, I also told him that being elected as a member of the board of a charity is not just an honour; it also brings with it certain duties, and a great amount of responsibility.

I had known John to be a hard working, honest and ethical person. He was not the "dog-eat-dog" type of business person who would consider cutting corners to reduce his construction costs. I also knew that he was concerned for those who worked for him. He also understood his responsibility to share his resources with others, including the less fortunate of this world. John told me that when he began is construction business, he adopted a mission statement for his company which said simply: "We honour God and value people in every construction job we undertake."

Previously, John had shared some things which convinced me that he took his company's mission statement seriously. For example, I know that he lost some construction jobs early in his company's history because he insisted on providing nothing but top grade materials and workmanship. I also know that, although he expected a hard day's work from his employees, he paid them well. He also saw to it that his employees would be rewarded for their contributions to the growth of the company. From the beginning, he had made the commitment that the company's before tax profits would be split four ways. Twenty-five percent would go to charity, another twenty-five percent would go into a reserve fund to pay employees in tough economic times, a further twenty-five percent would be paid out as annual bonuses to the employees, including himself, and the final twenty-five percent would be used to build and expand the company.

I knew that John had built his business on the basis of principles and that his business had prospered as a result. I also told him that I was sure that there were things he had done in the past which he would do differently if he had been in possession of the correct and complete information when he was faced with making decisions. But, such complete and accurate information is not always available.

John had looked at me somewhat skeptical. He wondered what I was getting at. He said that I made it sound as if he should be on guard now that he had become a member of the board of a major charity. Was I suggesting that his election to the board of directors of that charity was not just a recognition and an honour; a sort of reward for good corporate citizenship?

I told him that I would not deny that those elements probably were some of the reasons why he had been elected to the board of directors. But, that I have spent most of my working life in the charitable sector which had taught me a few things about the duties and responsibilities of a charity's board members. I told him that there are many things he should know about, when serving as a board member in charitable sector.

Serving on the board of a charity, I told him, is significantly different from making decisions for his own business, or any other profit making corporation. As a member of a charity's board, a director is called upon to make decisions for a public organization which exists exclusively for the benefit of the public. A relief and development agency is not just an organization which performs good deeds in far away places; such an organization is also a charity. A charity is a public trust. Every board member is responsible and accountable for the public's interest in the charity and its activities.

John wondered if I wasn't overemphasizing the responsibility and accountability part. The relief and development organization had a president and other properly qualified administrative staff to look after all the various operations and departments. He argued that his position on the board of directors was simply a position of prestige. His function as board member only required him to attend a number of board meetings where goals were set and the activities of the president and his staff were reviewed.

John's history of service in the charitable sector included having been an elder of his local church. He had also previously served on the board of directors of a college. Apparently, he had never understood that serving as an elder, or serving on the board of the college should impose duties or created responsibilities towards anyone but the organization he served. No one had ever explained to him that, as a board member of a charity, he had been at minimum a fiduciary, and likely also a trustee of those organizations. (The concept of a *fiduciary* and *trustee* will be explained and discussed in later chapters.)

John's understanding of his responsibilities as a director was very limited. As far as his responsibilities to his church were concerned, he took the position that the pastor and his staff take care of all matters of operating the church. His understanding was that the elders should receive periodic reports from the senior pastor and his staff. The elders, as board members, had no other responsibilities. John viewed his duties and responsibilities, as a board member of his church, to be passive.

When he served on the board of directors of the college, there was a president. The president was hired to be responsible for the operations of the college. In John's view, the college ran similar to his private construction company. The president, John believed, had to make decisions and has to be the only responsible person, otherwise nothing gets done.

John's understanding in relation to the duties and responsibilities of charity board members is not unique. It has been my experience that the views expressed by John are common among charity board members. The common view among board members is that the professionals are hired by the board to take care of all, and are responsible for all, the day-to-day operations of the charity. In many cases, boards also expect the professionals to set the direction and mandate of the organization. That is especially the case in some denominations and independent churches. Such board members believe that boards are there to receive periodic and annual reports, and to ask some penetrating questions of the chief executive officer to make sure that he or she is doing his or her job. If the board determines that the CEO no longer does his or her job, then the board's task is to replace the CEO.

In this time of rapid change, the governance of charities is becoming more and more complex. The old view of being a board member, which John subscribed to, no longer holds. Boards of charities must remain abreast of tax laws and reporting requirements. They also must know their duties and responsibilities as board members under common law, and numerous federal, state or provincial laws.

There was a time when it was assumed that charities, especially those charities which were places of worship, were immune from many laws that apply to other organizations and corporations. It was argued by many that charities were involved in work for the general good of their members. But such a view is contrary to the common law of charity. After all, it is because charities operate for the public good, and not for the benefit of their members, that they enjoy tax exempt status and obtain favourable tax treatment for gifts made by their donors.

Over the last several decades, there has been an increase, in the demand for public accountability to the state or province. Constitutionally, in Canada, the regulation of charities is a provincial, as opposed to a federal, power. In the US, the situation is much the same. Generally the states are responsible for charities and their activities. The reason why only the federal government was visible in the regulation of charities was because of the tax exempt status of the organizations, and the tax benefits for charitable donations enjoyed by donors. It is now generally accepted that charities are also accountable to the public at large through the appropriate state and provincial authorities.

There are reasons for the government's and public's increased interest in charities. First of all, governments have an interest in the operation of charities because they are significant beneficiaries of tax incentives. Secondly, the public's increased interest is because there is a greater recognition developing that charities hold their resources exclusively for the benefit of the public, and not for the members of the organization.

Charities are exempt from income tax on their income. In addition, those who support charities, by means of a voluntary transfer of money, or other tangible property, without valuable consideration, are entitled to either deduct the value of their gifts from their taxable income or to receive a tax credit.

Some governments view such benefits either as foregone tax revenue or as tax expenditures. Such governments, therefore, want to make sure that the publicly assisted resources of charities are used for purposes which are for the public good.

Governments did not always view the exemption of income tax on gifts made to charities as foregone taxes, or tax expenditures. The foregone taxes, or tax expenditure concept has developed since the nineteen-sixties. The tax expenditure concept was a result of a basic shift in the understanding of property rights of individuals after World War II.

When taxation on the income of individuals and corporations was first introduced, it was understood that the private sector had a responsibility to share of their resources to pay for the services provided to the public by governments. Taxation of individuals and corporations, based on their disposable income, was considered to be a progressive form of taxation. Fundamental to this taxation approach was the philosophy that disposable income belonged to the individual or the corporation. The individual or corporation should pay their fair share of government services. Everyone paid tax on their disposable income, after making allowances for basic personal needs.

Since World War II, social and political theory has changed significantly. We have to see that change in the light of the strong Marxist influence when the current bureaucrats attended university. The current government mandarins were trained on the basis of the fundamental theory that all property belongs to the state. These bureaucrats believe that the state, exclusively, has the power to decide what property an individual or corporation may retain for private use.

The above distinction may be interesting from a social philosophy point of view, but in the end, it needs to be determined whether the tax expenditure concept really makes a difference. I believe that the fundamental philosophical approach to property rights makes a significant difference. A specific Canadian example may help to illustrate that difference.

Prior to 1989, both individuals and corporations were entitled to deduct, from their taxable income, gifts made to charitable organizations up to twenty percent of net income. The theory was that amounts given to charities were not available as disposable income for personal or corporate use. Therefore, it would not be appropriate to include such amounts in establishing income tax to be paid.

After 1988, tax law was changed to provide for a tax credit for gifts made by individuals to charities recognized under the *Income Tax Act, Canada*. Under the new approach, individuals, who would pay income tax at the lower marginal tax rates, receive tax credits at the highest personal tax rate, when they make annual gifts above a minimum dollar amount. The tax credit for the minimum annual amount of gifts is at the lowest personal marginal tax rate.

At the present time, the Canadian government indirectly spends tax money on those donors who normally pay income tax at the lower personal marginal tax rates. For example, a Canadian earning less that $29,000, who gives a total amount of $3,000 to charity, receives a federal tax credit of $846 under the new system. Under the old system, that same individual would have paid lower federal income tax of about $510. The actual tax expenditure cost to the federal government is about $336.

This actual cost to the federal government is a significant difference. Therefore, recent language in information coming from the Canadian Department of Finance speaks of "tax assistance for charitable donations." This is a clear change from the old language rooted in the concept of a reduction in disposable income.

But it may still be argued that this difference may not be significant from the point of view of the charity itself. The response to such arguments is that the government can accept the actual cost of the expenditure only because it views both the income deduction, and the tax credit as an indirect expenditure by the government. Once you accept the tax expenditure theory for all charitable gifts, you can decide to manipulate the level of these expenditures to meet current social and political policy objectives. What the government gives, the government can take away.

The point can be made that the right to reduce income by the amount of charitable gifts, within limits, is subject to the same change. The Canadian government could just as well increase or decrease the percentage of gifts in relation to net income which could be deducted under the old system. However, there is a significant difference. Once you legislate the tax expenditure concept into the taxation system, both the government and the public – not just the donors – have the right to demand an accounting of and, at least in theory, a say in how a charity's resources are spent.

Let me try to make my concern a little more clear by using an imaginary example. Under the Constitution of the United States of America, the separation between church and state doctrine has evolved to the extent that it is considered inappropriate for tax funds to be used for any type of religious purpose or activity. What do you think the result would be if the tax expenditure concept would be written into United States tax law?

The Supreme Court of the United States of America could take one of two approaches to this issue. Either the Court would decide that such a tax law is unconstitutional because it results in the state supporting religion, or, as an alternative course of action, the Court could decide that gifts to places of worship will no longer be eligible for such favourable tax treatment.

In the first alternative course of action, the Supreme Court would confirm the private property rights of disposable income. In the second alternative, the Court would accept the public property rights of disposable income, but at the same time would remove gifts to places of worship from eligibility for tax deduction.

I am afraid that sooner or later there will be public pressure placed on the Canadian government to remove the "advancement of religion" purpose as a valid charitable purpose. The argument will be that the government has no business supporting any religion with either direct or indirect tax funds. That could result in a significant reduction in gifts to the church, especially in relation to bequests.

If such a drastic change would take place there would be a significant shift in activities undertaken by many religious charities. Many churches are now involved in activities which could be classified under the other three headings of charity, i.e. the relief of poverty, the advancement of education, or some form of social services. In the end, only donors to places of worship would be denied the right to a tax credit or deduction from income for their gifts.

This change is not likely to happen in the near future. If it happens, it will take some time. The Roman Catholic Church and protestant mainline churches still have enough political influence to prevent such an action in the near future. But churches and other religious charities should resist asking the government for more tax incentives for charitable gifts.

The reason that the public takes a direct interest in the activities of charities is because the resources received by charities have a public trust attached to them. Under both state and provincial law, gifts received by a charity must be used for the benefit of the public in general and cannot be used for private purposes. The attorney generals' departments of both states and provinces are responsible to represent the public interest, and to supervise charities to make sure that charitable funds are used exclusively for charitable purposes.

This book deals with some of the major issues that charity board members face. The duties and responsibilities to which board members of charities are exposed, and which they take upon themselves, are considered in some detail. Further, I have provided board members of charities with some practical policy development discussions on some of the issues faced by most charities. Finally, at the end of each chapter, I have included a list of questions and statements. The responses to the questions and statements can be used to evaluate the performance and effectiveness of a charity and its governing board in light of the duties and responsibilities discussed in each chapter. It is my hope that they will help board members to evaluate their personal performance and the effectiveness of the charities they serve. I have also included an appendix at the end of the book to be used by board members to perform an internal evaluation of the charity.

ONE

The Charitable Gift

In this chapter, we want to concentrate on what makes a payment to a charity a "gift." We will look at the elements that must be present when a donor transfers property, usually money, to a charity before the donor can claim the transfer as a gift for income tax purposes. We will also take a look at what restrictions are imposed on charities for accepting designated gifts. We will see that a charity may not be in a position to accept every designated donation that is offered to it.

The "gift"

When a person makes a donation to a charity, such a payment must meet the test of charitable purposes if the donor wishes to claim a deduction or tax credit for making the donation. Neither Canada's *Income Tax Act*, nor the United States of America's *Internal Revenue Code* define the word *gift*. The courts, over many centuries of common law tradition, have determined that a gift is "the voluntary transfer of property without valuable consideration." This means that a donor must, irrevocably, transfer all rights in the property to the charity, without any remaining "strings attached," if the donor wishes to claim the transfer of the property, usually money, for income deduction or tax credit purposes.

If the donor retains any right, even one as simple as the donor's right to direct the use of a gift at a later date, then it could be argued that a "consideration" remains attached to the gift; namely, the right to decide the use to which the gift may be put in the future. Retention of such a right, in law, could make the transfer of property partially revocable and, therefore, it may not meet the strict legal definition of a gift for income tax purposes.

Some people will argue that I exaggerate the future direction of a gift issue. They will argue that the issue never arises in the real world. Most people will say that they have never made a gift to a charity with the stipulation that they want to tell the organization how to use the gift in the future. If people don't trust the organization's ability to use the gifts wisely, they won't make a gift to that organization.

Redesignating a prior gift

But the problem of redesignating gifts at some time after the donation was made happens more frequently and more innocently than one would think. For example, let's assume that a donor makes a gift to an international relief and development organization and stipulates that the gift is to be used for disaster relief in a developing country which is politically unstable. Let's further assume that the government of the designated country is removed by internal revolt, and that a long period of dictatorship begins during which time relief agencies and their representatives are no longer welcome. In such a situation, the organization would not be able to use the donor's gift for the designated purpose. Who, then, is able to determine an alternative use for the gift?

Such an alternative use for the gift cannot be determined by the original donor. The original donor transferred the funds with all the rights of property attached to the gift. To approach the donor for redirection of the gift would be to acknowledge that the gift had not been irrevocable without any residual rights. Therefore, to approach the donor for the right to redirect the gift could cause the transfer of property to fail as a gift for income tax purposes.

Such an alternative use of the gift also cannot be determined by the charity. The charity accepted the gift with all the rights and restrictions that were attached to it. Under trust law, the charity cannot change any of the rights or restrictions that it accepted when it received the transfer of property from the donor. The charity is the trustee of such a designated gift and must see to it that the property is used for the designated purpose.

Let me try to make this concept a little more clear by an example with similar considerations.

A charity is in a situation similar to an executor or administrator of an estate. If the designated purpose prescribed by the testator (the person who is disposing of his assets accumulated during his or her lifetime by means of a will) no longer can be carried out by the executor or the administrator of the estate, the issue must be referred to the court for a change in the testator's will.

The same situation applies to a charity which accepts gifts restricted for a particular purpose. Neither the executor or administrator of a will, nor the administration or the board of a charity has the power to change the terms of the gift. And, neither the executor or administrator of a will, nor the administrators or the board of a charity can go back to the donor for direction to charge the terms of the gift. In the case of the testator, that may appear obvious since the testator must be deceased when the will is executed. However, the donor to a charity actually is in the same position as the deceased testator in relation to a charitable gift. The donor has relinquished all rights in the property transferred to the charity and, therefore, is in a position similar to the deceased when property is irrevocably given to a charity.

The problem indicated by the above example is that the charity never truly received exclusive control over the money it had received from the donor. The gift was received in trust for a specific purpose. There is nothing wrong with a charity receiving a gift for a specific purpose as long as the charity at the same time receives the right to redirect the gift for other similar purposes, if the need for the original purpose no longer exists.

Charities can avoid the potential problems which can arise out of receiving designated gifts. To accomplish this, the charity should include a special notice to every gift appeal. This notice should say that:

"The charity solicits your gifts for the purpose identified in this appeal. However, if the project for which the gifts are received has been fully funded or cannot be completed for reasons beyond the control of the charity, the board reserves the right to use such funds for other similar projects."

Designated bequests

Let me give another illustration of how gifts are at times designated.

Some time ago I was informed that a church had received a substantial bequest for a specific purpose. The purpose was to install bells in the church steeple.

The church had never decided that such an expenditure should be made. When the church board investigated the cost of such a project, it was discovered that the gift they had accepted would not cover even half of the total cost of installing the bells. At an official meeting of the church board, it was decided that the installation of church bells was not in accordance with the church's current or long range plans. Therefore, a resolution was passed not to install the bells.

At this point, the church had a problem which, at first, it did not recognize. The church had accepted a substantial amount of money for a project which the church did not adopt as its purpose. The church board decided to put the gift aside for a future project. However, the problem was that the church had not received the right to redesignate the use of the gift.

The net result of this situation is that the church would have to apply to the court to have the purpose of the bequest changed. This is an expensive procedure which the church had to pay for out of its other charitable resources.

It is difficult for a charity to prevent the specific designation of a bequest. Charities usually do not know that a bequest may be coming before a will is read or probated after the donor's death. But a charity can take one action to reduce the incidence of receiving a bequest which does not fit the charity's purposes. A charity should have a general bequest brochure which it distributes to its members and donors. This brochure should include information which will inform potential donors of the legal problems which can arise if a donor designates a bequest for a purpose that has not been approved by the charity.

In the case of a bequest to the church for the installation of bells in the church tower, the church should have notified the executor of the estate that it could not accept the gift with that restriction attached. If the church had done that, the executor would have been required to make application to the court for the change in specific purpose. In such a situation, the cost of the application would have been paid for by the estate.

Endowment funds

Many charities place their bequests in endowment funds. Other charities establish endowment funds to secure a regular income stream in the future. Charitable organizations need to determine whether endowment funds are appropriate for their organizations. Should a charity wish to, or be allowed to, accumulate funds which will *never* be used for charitable purposes? Is such an accumulation of funds in accordance with the charity's mandate to spend its resources exclusively for charitable purposes? Is it appropriate for governments to allow persons a deduction from income, or tax credits, for money contributed to charities when the actual funds will not be used for charitable purposes, either now or in the future? The following brief analysis will address these questions.

Endowment funds are normally established from two sources. One source of endowment funds is money designated by the board as surplus to current needs. The other source of endowment funds is money designated by donors, either through bequests, or by means of restricted current gifts. The objective of an endowment fund is to hold the capital, either for a specific number of years, or in perpetuity. Normally, only the income generated by the invested endowment funds is used for the charity's charitable purposes.

If the governing board designates certain funds as endowment funds, the board also has the authority to return such funds back to the operating fund. If the donor, by means of a bequest or designation, restricts the endowment fund, the terms of the designation have to be followed.

Donors can restrict the use of capital contributed to an endowment fund for whatever length of time they choose. Frequently, donors wish to restrict the use of the capital contributed to the endowment fund in perpetuity. One motivation for such a restriction could be that the donor believes that the charity should have income in the future, independent of gift income from the then current sources. Another motivation on the part of the donor might be that the donor wishes to have his or her name attached to the fund for all time to come. In this way some donors believe that they will be remembered by the charity and the beneficiaries of the endowment fund – they wish to guarantee themselves a form of immortality.

Charities need to address certain ethical questions before they agree to establish endowment funds. There are few, if any, concerns if a donor wishes to establish an endowment fund for a specific number of years. However, when a donor wishes to establish an endowment fund in perpetuity, a number of issues need to be addressed. For example, let us assume that a donor to a charity, dedicated to eradicating a specific disease, wishes to establish a perpetual endowment fund. Should that charity accept such a perpetual endowment fund? The charity is dedicated to spending all funds received in pursuit of its charitable purpose – the eradication of a disease. By establishing or accepting endowment funds, the charity gives one of two messages: either the charity does not believe that it will be successful in eradicating the disease, or the charity gives the message that using all of its resources to eradicate the disease is not its sole objective – a strange, but logical conclusion indeed.

There are other organizations that should have great difficulty in accepting permanent endowment funds. One such organization would a Christian church. A Christian church exists to advance religion for the sole purpose of preparing people for the time when the current order of things will end; when "all believers will be taken up into glory." It would seem to be incompatible with the mission of a church to accept permanent endowment funds. The mission of the church is to devote all of its resources on current evangelism or missions. To accept money which must be kept in perpetuity would appear to be at odds with such a mission.

There is another reason why perpetual endowment funds should be questioned. Donors to charities receive favourable tax treatment for such gifts. The reason for such favourable treatment is that the gifts are used for the benefit of the public. Charitable gifts are a sort of voluntary tax for the public good. However, gifts to be held in perpetuity as endowment funds will never be used for the benefit of the public. Are such gifts truly charitable? Should there not be a law against perpetuities for endowment trusts operated by a charity in the same way that there is a law against perpetuity for all other types of trusts?

Are board members trustees?

Because of the situation which I have just explained, among others, there are strong arguments that board members of charities in Canada and the United States of America are trustees of the gifts entrusted to them. Both countries have a legal system based on the British common law tradition.

Board members of charities have duties and responsibilities at least equal to directors and officers of for-profit corporations. In addition they have added responsibilities imposed on them by common law.

Although the concept of charities holding their resources in trust for the benefit of the public has been more or less accepted, the recognition that board members of charities effectively are trustees of the charity's gift receipts has come into focus in Canada only since *The Toronto Humane Society, Public Trustee v. The Toronto Humane Society and T. Robert Humbley* case. In that case, the controlling board members of the society had paid themselves salaries as officers, using charitable funds for that purpose. The court decided that a charitable organization is answerable for its activities, and the disposition of its property, as though the charity was a trustee.

Some legal experts in Canada have concluded that this trustee concept only applies in the province of Ontario, where the *Charities Accounting Act* specifically states that: any "corporation incorporated for a religious, educational, charitable, or public purpose shall be deemed to be a trustee within the meaning of this Act... and any real or personal property acquired by it shall be deemed to be property within the meaning of this Act." These legal experts maintain that board members of charities are bound only by the rules which affect trustees, but that they are not trustees in the true sense of the word. On that basis, they argue that board members of charities are fiduciaries, i.e. they act on behalf of others, the public, to whom they owe their duties and complete allegiance without self-interest.

There are other legal experts who believe that trusteeship for board members of charities is based on common law rather than specific legislation. Those legal experts believe that all donations made to a charity are a public trust. This places a responsibility on the board members of a charity to deal with such public trusts in a way which goes beyond the responsibilities of a fiduciary. Such legal experts believe that board members of charitable organizations are in fact trustees. They maintain that the trust concept is not limited to those Ontario charities and their governing boards which are incorporated and which are, therefore, accountable under the above quoted section of the *Charities Accounting Act*, but that it also applies equally to unincorporated charities.

It should be noted that, although there is a distinction between board members of charitable organizations being held to be fiduciaries, as opposed to trustees, such a distinction applies only in the level of legal defence available to the board members. Under the fiduciary concept, board members are able to raise the defence that they were inactive and did not participate in the particular offending decision. Trustees, on the other hand, are liable if they fail to supervise the actions of their fellow trustees.

The final determination as to whether board members of charities are fiduciaries only, or if they are also trustees will have to wait until further case law develops. In time other provinces and states will have to deal with this question. The Public Guardian and Trustee of Ontario considers the governing boards of charities, both incorporated and unincorporated, to be made up of trustees. The Public Guardian and Trustee of Ontario believes that such a position has a sound basis in common law.

Responsibilities if board members are trustees

In the Introduction to this book, I said that many board members of charities consider their responsibilities to be satisfied as long as they rigorously supervise the activities of the administration. That position may be sound if, in fact, board members are fiduciaries without the additional duties being imposed on them because they are also considered to be trustees. The courts likely will continue to develop the concept of a greater responsibility for charity board members by saddling them with duties equal to those of trustees. Even if they stop short of declaring board members of charities to be trustees, the courts likely will require the higher trustee accountability in any case.

Let's look at an example of the difference between being a fiduciary and a trustee. An individual has immediate family members working for the charity of which the individual is a board member. The question is whether salary payments made to the board member's immediate family members can be distinguished from the payments made to the officers of the Toronto Humane Society discussed earlier.

At first glance, there seems to be a rather obvious difference. In the Toronto Humane Society case, the officers were themselves directors. So there is an element of self-dealing which is objectionable under the Ontario legislation. But, even if we accept the suggestion that the courts in other jurisdictions will adopt a position similar to the Toronto Humane Society case, then salary payments by a charity to immediate family members would seem to be far different than self-dealing. The board member does not receive a personal financial benefit – either directly or indirectly – from the salaries received by immediate family members.

This argument may be valid, but we should wait with attempting to answer that issue until we have looked at all the duties of board members as fiduciaries and trustees. But before we deal with that issue, we want to take a look at some other issues affecting the treatment of gifts to charities.

Fundraising inducements

As stated above, a donation, to qualify as a gift for income tax purposes, must meet two tests. The first test is that the payment must be made voluntarily. The second test is that the payment must be without consideration having any commercial value.

There are many charities which provide donors with inducements to make a gift in support of charitable purposes. Such inducements may range from items with nominal value, to items which have substantial value. Taxation authorities in both the United States of America and Canada have accepted that inducements of no significant commercial value, such as lapel pins, are a well established part of the fundraising landscape. Such "trinkets" are more a confirmation of belonging to a group than an indication that something of value was transferred to the donor.

In recent times, however, some charities have pushed the envelope over the line. There have been cases where items of significant commercial value have been offered to donors in return for a donation which would exceed a certain amount. For example, I have seen situations on both sides of the border where the charity offers a discount for services to its members. I have also seen situations where a charity will offer donors gifts of books or artistic prints, which have established retail values in commercial outlets, in return for a donation which is equal to, or greater than, the known retail value of the item received in return.

Split receipting

The practice of making inducement gifts, which have some commercial value, has come under scrutiny in Canada over the past decade. Revenue Canada has given directions that must be used in calculating the gift portion in such fundraising practices. Revenue Canada's IT-110R3 restricts charities from issuing official receipts in situations where the fair market value of the inducement exceeds the lesser of $50.00 or 10% of the amount of the gift. Fair market value is the price for which the item is available to the general public through established commercial outlets. For example, a charity may be able to purchase a large quantity of books from a publisher because the purchase is the publisher's remainder of a print run. As a result, the charity may pay as little as 30% of the retail price that a book store would charge its customers. In such a situation, the inducement value of the book is not the cost of the book to the charity, but the price for which the book normally sells in book stores.

The reason why Revenue Canada introduced the formula is because no official receipt could have been issued by a Canadian registered charity without such a relieving provision. An official receipt for a combined payment, consisting of a payment for a service or product and a donation, is not acceptable in Canada. The only exception is in situations where Revenue Canada has issued either an Information Circular or an Interpretation Bulletin. The way Canadian law has developed is that the total payment is denied as a gift if any portion of it can be related to a direct or indirect benefit received by the donor. However, there are some exceptions. Receipts may be issued for contributions in excess of the fair market value of the meal consumed by donors at a fundraising dinner. A receipt may also be given for the gift portion of a payment for a charitable gift annuity. As noted above, a receipt may be given for the inducement returned to the donor to encourage the donor to make a gift when the value of the inducement is within the published restrictions. Finally, receipts are allowed for payment to a religious school by parents or guardians for the portion of such payments which are above the calculated "secular" education cost per pupil. In all other cases, the charity risks having its registration number revoked for issuing receipts which include amounts for which the donor has directly or indirectly received goods or services from the charity, which have a measurable commercial value for the donor.

In the United States of America, the situation is different. There the charity issues a receipt for all contributions received above a prescribed amount, but such a receipt is not a receipt which has a content prescribed by an act or regulations. Therefore, it is the donor who must determine the portion of any contribution which he or she may claim as a charitable gift to reduce his or her taxable income. Furthermore, in the United States of America, the law allows split receipting. The charity may issue the donor a receipt which identifies the portion of any payment, or series of payments, that relates to a product or service received by the donor from the charity, and the portion which relates to pure gifts. In this approach the charity is not at risk of losing its status because of incorrect receipting practices.

Deputized fundraising

In many situations it is difficult to determine when a direct or indirect benefit has been received by a donor. There have been instances where the taxation authorities on both sides of the border have questioned the validity of a gift where the donor did not benefit from the gift, but where a linkage was perceived to exist between the donor and a person who was the beneficiary of the charity's services.

In the case of one charity, the Internal Revenue Service refused to provide a charity tax exempt status because the charity used what has been called "deputized fundraising" methods. Deputized fundraising means that an individual, usually a missionary who hopes to be sent abroad, is required to raise support for the organization. This method of fundraising is used to assure the organization that there will be sufficient funds for the organization to pay for the support of the individual during his or her term of appointment. The process in such deputized fundraising is that the individual must meet all the appointment requirements before being sent out to raise funds for the charity. When all the requirements for appointment have been met, the individual is "deputized" or declared ready to be sent out except for the level of financial support that he or she has to raise in support of the organization. At this point the individual is sent out on behalf of the organization to raise gift commitments to meet the organization's expenditures for the term of appointment. To be able to show that the deputized person had raised the required amount of gift commitments, donors would be asked to indicate to the organization that their gifts were in support of the individual's work for the organization. This practice of deputized fundraising has a long history in religious organizations.

The reason that the Internal Revenue Service refused to give tax exempt status to the charity was because donors to a charity which has received such status may deduct gifts made to such a charity from their taxable income. The Internal Revenue Service was concerned that donors who gave money in support of a particular individual were involved in acts of private benevolence.

Private vs. public benevolence

Private benevolence occurs when an individual gives money to another person selected by the individual personally. For example, if I run into a poor person in one of the inner cities of North America and give such a person a five dollar bill, the act of giving is charity. However, because I make a personal decision about the poor person's need, the act of charity on my part is not a gift for income tax purposes.

Over many centuries of common law, the principle has been well established that an organization which operates at arms-length from the donor must make the determination whether an act of charity is charitable for income tax purposes. The courts have determined that acts of charity must be available to the public at large. If the group served by the organization is so restrictive that the public at large could not benefit, the acts of charity of such an organization also would be classified as private benevolence. Such an organization would not be able to obtain tax exempt charitable status or registration on either side of the border. Consequently, donors to such an organization would not be entitled to the beneficial tax treatment for their donations. To be eligible for the favourable tax treatment, the donor must relinquish control over gifts to a charity. If the charity does not receive exclusive control over the money donated, it is not a gift. This transfer of control over the funds donated to the charity is the first test to determine whether a donation is private or public benevolence.

To meet the second test of eligibility for the beneficial income tax treatment under law, the charitable activities of the organization must also be available to the public as opposed to a narrow interest group. This does not mean that all the charity's funds or services must be provided to the public as a whole. The public benefit test will have been met when all members of the public can have access to the goods or services provided by the organization. For example, an organization which restricts its services exclusively to employees of one company would not be considered a public benevolence charity. It is not possible for all members of the community to become employees of one corporation. However, the benefits of a charitable organization can be restricted to students of a particular school provided that enrollment in such a school is open to all members of the community who meet the general requirements such as age and academic aptitude, or ability.

The distinction between acts of private and public benevolence on the part of charitable organizations is not always black and white. For that reason, the taxation authorities take great care to determine, not only that the objects of the organization are exclusively charitable in law, but also, that the activities of the organization meet the test of public benevolence. Both the status letter, or registration process, and the subsequent audits were put in place to monitor the activities of charities to make sure that they comply with the common law requirements.

To summarize, the beneficial income tax treatment for donations to charity must meet the test that: firstly, control over the donated funds is transferred to the charity exclusively; and secondly, that the funds are used by the charity for the benefit of the public.

Deputized fundraising and public benevolence

The above discussion may lead some to conclude that the Internal Revenue Service was correct in not giving the charity which practiced "deputized fundraising" its charitable status. At first glance, there might be some logic in that position. After all, the deputized fundraisers solicit support so that they can be assured that funds will be available to them for their salaries, and for other project expenditures once they leave on their foreign assignments. However, the designated fundraising program does not allow the donor to retain control over the donated funds.

The charity determined that the fundraisers should be deputized for their service abroad as employees of the charity. The charity had exclusive control, either to appoint or not to appoint the individual to become deputized. In addition, the charitable purpose of the charity is not the payment of salary or benefits to the deputized individual, but to make use of the deputized individual's services to implement the charity's charitable purposes abroad. The deputized fundraiser is not the beneficiary of charity; rather he or she delivers charitable benefits to others in the field.

Designation and private benevolence

It is incorrect to conclude that funds designated by donors for a particular project or service, within the charitable purposes of a charity, are tainted by private benevolence. As long as the charity selects the projects and selects the people who will benefit from its services, the charity is in control of its resources. Designating donations for a charity's specific projects or purposes has long been a method used to encourage donors who identify with such projects or services. For example, child sponsorship programs of charities have successfully used this method to obtain long-term donation commitments from donors. They have obtained such long-term commitments by encouraging a certain level of interaction between a child who is selected by the charity with a donor to that charity. The donor will be encouraged to "sponsor" a child by making a fixed monthly donation to the charity. When the donor makes such a commitment, he or she receives a picture of a child, some family or general information and the address where the donor can send letters addressed to the child.

In the child sponsorship programs, the donor does not select the child. The selection is done exclusively by the charity. The donor's gift dollars do not go to that child on a monthly basis. The gifts of all donors to child sponsorship programs are pooled. The amount requested from donors is the average amount it costs to provide the needed assistance for all children in the program. As a matter of fact, much of the support in a child sponsorship program may not even go to the child personally. If the living conditions in a village are such that they need to be improved to be able to help the needy children in such a village, the child sponsorship charity may undertake a project such as drilling a well. Providing a community with clean drinking water benefits the sponsored child, as well as the total community in which the child lives.

I have known of situations, where donors have established such long-term relationships with sponsored children, that such sponsors have visited the sponsored child. In some cases, the bonds of relationship have developed to such an extent that "adoption" of a child has taken place. Adoption in such instances does not mean that the child is removed out of his or her existing family, and moved to North America. However, it does mean that the sponsor becomes something like a "god-parent" to the child.

Strong ties between the donor and the beneficiary of the child sponsorship charity have led some to question whether the donor has not crossed the line from public benevolence to private benevolence when the donor's gifts are made to the child sponsorship charity. My response to such questions is that the donor neither selected the child, nor do the donor's gifts either directly or indirectly go exclusively to the sponsored child. The sponsored child is simply a proportionate beneficiary of the pooled gifts from all donors.

Just because close ties are established between an "arms length" donor and a sponsored child does not make the gift from the donor to the charity, which supports the child, private benevolence. The charity continues to use the same criteria as before to determine the level of support needed by the child. The donor has no influence in this determination.

If the donor sends additional support, in whatever form, to a sponsored child, such additional support is private benevolence. However, it is my belief that the monthly amounts donated to the charity remain public benevolence no matter what type of relationship may develop between the donor and the sponsored child in the future.

Detached, disinterested generosity

Over the past few decades a new concept has entered the charitable lexicon. This concept is that a gift to be eligible for the beneficial tax treatment must be made out of a "detached, disinterested generosity." This concept was first used in the High Court of Australia. The High Court stated that a donor could not receive any form of direct or indirect benefit as a result of the gift. The same concept was also referred to in a case in the United States of America.

The difficulty with introducing this new concept is that it places much charitable giving in question. The courts, by introducing such new language, without clear definition of its meaning, have drawn into question gifts made by individuals who may directly, or indirectly benefit from the services of a charity. If this concept means what the dictionary definitions of the words appear to mean, can a person who has a specific disease donate to a charity dedicated to eradicating that disease? Can a person who is an alumnus of a college or university make a donation to his or her Alma matter? Can members of cultural charities such as a symphony, a theatre or a museum donate to such a charity and receive beneficial tax treatment for their gifts when they file their income tax returns?

The High Court in Australia, in subsequent cases, has provided some clarification of what it meant by the "detached, disinterested generosity" concept. The High Court stated that the concept does not apply in situations where a donor would not be required to make a payment to the beneficiary of charity if the charity did not support such individual. For example, if a donor is legally required to make a payment to the sponsored child in a situation where the child sponsorship charity does not support the child, then the concept applies. With the High Court's current definition of the concept, it is doubtful that it means anything more than the old, well defined concept that a gift must be "a voluntary transfer of property without valuable consideration."

The difficulty is that the Internal Revenue Service and Revenue Canada seem to be testing how far they can take the "detached, disinterested generosity" concept in their respective jurisdictions. The denial to register the charity involved in "deputized fundraising" by the Internal Revenue Service would appear to be related to this concept. Certain gifts which are being questioned by Revenue Canada in relation to child sponsorship programs, and missionary support to individuals related to donors, appear to be based on the same concept. It is hoped that some clarity will be restored in the future.

The unfortunate situation for the charitable sector is that the "detached, disinterested generosity" concept will be very costly for that sector until its meaning is clarified. The costs will come from two directions. The charitable sector will have to pay high legal costs to defend Internal Revenue Service or Revenue Canada challenges to both charities and donors. At the same time, because of the profile of such legal cases, the public will become aware of the issues and reduce donations to charity. This reduction in donations will result if there is even a remote chance that donors will be linked to a benefit from charity as a result of their gifts.

I am aware of one generous chartered accountant who has written a charity dedicated to eliminate diabetes that he can no longer support that charity because he is a diabetic. This donor will withhold his gifts until the issue is resolved. The government of Canada must provide a clear legal definition of the word "gift" to include situations where a donor may receive an indirect, non-material benefit from the charity. Alternatively, the courts must resolve that "detached, disinterested generosity" does not mean that an indirect, non-material beneficiary of charity may not donate to such a charity.

It would appear prudent, on the part of every charity and every board member of a charity in both the United States of America and Canada, to make the Internal Revenue Service and Revenue Canada officials aware of the problems created by their "detached, disinterested generosity" concept. If that concerted action does not change the minds of the taxation authorities, charities, their board members and their donors may have to lobby their elected representatives for legislative changes. If the elected representatives do not act decisively by making it clear that indirect, non-material benefits are acceptable for donations to qualify as "gifts" for income tax purposes, there may be a significant decline in charitable services. Until this issue is resolved, charities may have to direct many of their resources to legal actions, and donors may be uncertain as to which charities they may support without challenge.

I have yet to speak to a donor who believes that he or she has ever made a gift out of a "detached, disinterested generosity." The dictionary meanings of these words are an oxymoron for all donors who take their donations seriously. Such donors maintain that it would be irresponsible to support a charity in which they had no interest.

Valuable consideration means that any benefit received must be measurable in commercial terms. Therefore, a donor to a symphony who receives a free ticket to a performance of the symphony after he has made the gift may use the receipt for income tax purposes, provided that he or she did not know that the free ticket would be received when a gift was made. However, a donor who is induced to make a gift of a certain amount with the clear understanding that free books will be available because of the gift, has entered into a commercial transaction. In Canada, the total gift will be tainted by the commercial element, and, therefore, ineligible for income tax purposes. In the United States of America, the fair market value of the consideration received would have to be deducted from the gift for income tax purposes.

Conclusion on gift issues

The discussions in this chapter do not address all the issues which a charity and its board members may face in relation to what constitutes valid charitable gifts. However, the foregoing discussions will provide all board members with sufficient understanding of the underlying principles to be able to determine when a payment should be treated as a gift, and when it should be treated as a payment for goods or services received, which are of a material nature and measurable in commercial terms. Until the true meaning of the concept "detached, disinterested generosity" has been determined, or until the meaning of the word "gift" has been codified in legislation, charities should continue to use the old legal concept that a gift is a "voluntary transfer of property, without valuable consideration."

To make sure that both the charity and its board members are in compliance with the legal requirement relating to "gifts" to charities, it is important that receipting policies and procedures be reviewed on a regular basis. Below are a number of questions that should be answered at least on an annual basis. Board members who take such precautionary measures likely will escape any liabilities arising from inadvertent errors.

Questions for consideration

To make sure that your organization follows correct receipting practices, the following questions, or statements, should all be able to be answered with a "yes." If any question is answered "no," the practice to which it relates should be reviewed. Although board members, especially of larger organizations, may not be involved in the day-to-day activities of the charity, they should exercise supervision over the staff to make sure that all receipting is done in accordance with the law.

1. Does the board have a clearly defined, written fund raising policy?   ___yes ___no

2. Does the board have a clearly defined, written donor designation policy which is communicated in all fund raising appeals?

    ___yes ___no

3. The organization does not accept donor designated gifts or bequests unless the purpose for which the donation or bequest has been received has received prior approval by the board.

    ___yes ___no

4. The organization never issues receipts for income tax purposes for a payment when part or all of the payment is for goods or services unless specifically authorized by the appropriate taxing authority.

    ___yes ___no

5. The organization never issues a receipt for income tax purposes when a gift is designated for the benefit of a specific person.

    ___yes ___no

6. If your charity currently has, or plans to have, endowment funds, are such funds appropriate for your charity?

    ___yes ___no

7. Does the organization annually appoint an external auditor?

    ___yes ___no

8. Does the organization make its financial statements available to the public upon written request?

    ___yes ___no

Two

Organizing As a Charity

In this chapter we will discuss the various ways in which charities can be organized. Such a discussion may help to understand the different relationships and duties of board members to their organizations, to each other, and to other interested parties such as staff, clients, donors and the public at large.

Governing documents

It goes without saying that every charity, whether incorporated or unincorporated, must have governing documents. The simplest method of becoming established as a charity is by means of a Deed of Trust. The most complex is to be incorporated by special legislation passed by a province or state.

There are no exact statistics about the form of organization which is most common. I believe that the most common form of obtaining official status as a charity is by that of incorporation under the appropriate legislation of a state, province or the federal government. However, when churches are included, there are still many charities that are not incorporated.

Whatever the form of organization, every organization must apply for registration as a charity in Canada, or for tax exempt status in the United States of America. Once the registration or exemption status has been received, the charity is exempt from income tax. In addition, donors to the charity are then also entitled to claim gifts made to a charity as income deductions, or tax credits, on their annual income tax returns.

Being able to offer income tax deductions, or tax credits for donations, is a tremendous privilege which must be safeguarded and protected by the charity, its governing board and its administrators.

Advantages and disadvantages of different forms of organizing

There are advantages and disadvantages of each form of organizing. I intend to go into them in some detail. I will be discussing them in relation to the charitable issues to be considered.

If a charity operates as an unincorporated entity, the governing board and the members will have personal liability exposure for all activities carried out in the name of the charity. If a charity chooses to operate as a charitable trust, there will be no question that the members of the trust are trustees. As a consequence they will be subject to the standards, duties, and obligations imposed by law on trustees.

Many governing boards of charities believe they can avoid the high standards, duties, and obligations imposed on trustees; and, therefore, avoid personal liabilities if the organization is incorporated. Although there may be some protection for the directors and members by incorporating, recent developments in case law would indicate that the traditional corporate veil is beginning to be penetrated. As we will see later, the corporate veil does not exist at all in relation to a number of legal challenges which members of the governing board and the administrators of their charities may face.

Charitable purposes

The most important issue to consider when preparing or amending governing documents, is to take care that all the objects are charitable in law. A charity may obtain and retain its charitable status under the *Income Tax Act, Canada* and the *Internal Revenue Code* of the United States of America if all of its objects fall within one or more of the charitable purposes. The charitable purposes are *the relief of poverty, the advancement of religion, the advancement of education, and other purposes beneficial to the community as a whole, in a way which the law regards as charitable.*

Normally, there is not much confusion about the first two purposes; most people are of common mind when it comes to what constitutes "the relief of poverty" and "the advancement of religion."

Charitable registration or status has been available to churches in the United States of America and Canada, because of the "advancement of religion" heading. It is interesting to note that "advancement of religion" may include indoctrination in, and advocacy of, a specific religion or a set of doctrines. Churches and places of worship enjoy this unique treatment as charities which does not apply to charities organized primarily for other charitable purposes.

When it comes to the "advancement of education," the same broad application of the law does not apply. The courts have not made a distinction between the "advancement of religion" and "indoctrination." But they have developed a dividing line between "education" and "advocacy." The courts have assumed that education takes place when there is a search for truth which expands knowledge. They also have decided that advocacy takes place when a certain set of established truth, or knowledge, is promoted as superior to another set of truth, or knowledge.

For example, if one of an organization's objectives includes promoting a specific philosophy, or life-style, charitable registration, or status for such a charity under the heading of the "advancement of education" would likely be denied or revoked.

An organization which seeks to inform people about abortion, and in the process is perceived to advocate a change in public policy, will not receive charitable registration from Revenue Canada, or tax exempt status from the Internal Revenue Service.

This does not mean that the respective governments will deny charities all activities which could be labelled as political or advocacy. Both governments allow charities to support a political position intended for the improvement of education in general, but they do not allow any charity to support the program of a particular politician, or political party on educational issues. Some political activities are acceptable so long as they relate to a charity's stated objectives and so long as they are politically and socially correct.

The charitable purpose requiring most interpretation is "other purposes beneficial to the community, in a way which the law regards as charitable." Health and community social service agencies obtain their charitable registration, or status, under this heading.

Any organization involved in improving a situation, or condition, that is in the interest of the public at large, assuming that such an organization is not involved in any activities which the courts have ruled are not charitable (e.g. advocacy), should be successful in obtaining charitable registration from Revenue Canada, or status from the Internal Revenue Service under this fourth general heading.

To prevent potential difficulties, it is a good idea for all charities to have their objects or amendments of their objects reviewed by professionals before submitting them to any state, provincial or federal authority.

The Deed of Trust

The simplest and quickest way for a new organization to become established as a charity is to organize as an unincorporated society under a Deed of Trust. All that is required is for a minimum of three people to execute a trust document which is called the Deed of Trust. This document contains all the powers and restrictions of the trust. Such a Deed of Trust should contain specific elements. Let's look at each of these elements specifically.

The first element of a Deed of Trust is the declaration of trust. This section identifies all the trustees, describes that the trust will be used for charitable purposes, and gives the name by which the trust will be known.

Although not required, there usually is a section which deals with the meaning of key words used in the document. It will also state that the Deed of Trust will be interpreted in accordance with the laws of a specific jurisdiction.

A trust deed, in order to be accepted as a charitable trust, must have a section describing the objects of the trust. The objects must be charitable under one, or more, of the common law headings for charitable purposes.

The taxation authorities will require a section which identifies where the organization's principal offices are located.

One of the sections must outline the powers and duties of the trustees. Without such a section in a charitable trust, the trustees would not be able to deal with the organization's resources.

It is also important to have a section which describes how decisions of the trustees are to be made, how a trustee may retire or removed, and how successor trustees may be appointed. This may include provision for a membership structure, which may require that new trustees are to be elected by, and from among, such members.

The Deed of Trust should also include a section which states how soon after the fiscal year-end financial statements will be prepared. It will also stipulate whether such statements should be audited by a professional accountant qualified to give audit opinions in the charity's state, or province, of jurisdiction.

Since a charitable trust is intended to exist for a long time, it is not possible to anticipate all the social, political, cultural and economic changes that may take place over time. Therefore, it is important that the Deed of Trust includes a section prescribing how the Deed of Trust may be amended, or terminated.

To be accepted as a charitable trust, the taxation authorities will require that the Deed of Trust precludes the resources of the trust to be used for the benefit of the trustees, members or settlor of the trust. Further, in case the trust is terminated, all the net assets of the trust must go to another organization with charitable status.

Restricted solely by law, and the Deed of Trust, the trustees of a charitable trust are able to do anything that directors of an incorporated charity are able to do.

The Deed of Trust type of charitable organization is the simplest and, therefore, the least expensive to organize. It is also the most expedient form of organizing. It should be remember that the members of such an organization do not have the protection of specific legislation which protects members of incorporated organizations.

Policy development under a Deed of Trust

Although the Deed of Trust has to contain all the governing information for the trust, there are additional rules or operating policies and procedures which the trustees may develop over time. The trustees should have the power to amend the Deed of Trust to include such new rules, or to develop operating policies and procedures.

Most charities organized under a Deed of Trust try to keep their primary governing document relatively brief and general. In this way it avoids the need for constant amendments. To refer to any additional rules, or operating policies and procedures that a charitable trust may have, as bylaws is inappropriate. A charity operating under a Deed of Trust is not incorporated. Therefore, such a document simply should be called the *Operating Policies and Procedures.*

The trustees must take care that any operating policies and procedures are within the mandate of the Deed of Trust. If proposed policies or procedures are not within the mandate of the Deed of Trust, the Deed of Trust itself must be amended.

One of the greatest problems with most charities organized by means of a Deed of Trust is that the trustees do not consult the Deed of Trust when they consider new activities or policies. This problem is not unique to charities organized under a Deed of Trust, but it is most common in this type of organization.

The members and trustees know that the Deed of Trust is a private document and that it is not government approved like an incorporating document. This gives the members, and trustees, the idea that the organization is not subject to legal restrictions. Therefore, the trustees believe that they can freely make any change they wish.

As long as the Deed of Trust allows the trustees to make changes to the trust, no one can stop the trustees from making any change, provided that the action does not itself breach, or destroy, the Deed of Trust. However, the trustees do not have the right to do something not specifically authorized by the Deed of Trust.

When the Deed of Trust is first executed, a copy of the trust document must be submitted with an application, and other prescribed information, to Revenue Canada or the Internal Revenue Service, in order to receive charitable registration, or status. When a Deed of Trust is amended, a copy of the amendment should be submitted to Revenue Canada or the Internal Revenue Service no later than the subsequent annual filing.

The taxation authorities are concerned with the tax-exempt status of the organization. They are also concerned with the income deductions or tax credits claimed by private donors to such organizations. The taxation authorities have no other reason for controlling the activities of charities. States and provinces should be concerned with the activities of charities, but they have shown little interest in charities until recently.

The Deed of Trust type of charitable organization can be used by any group wishing to establish a charity in Canada or the United States of America. Any group can organize in this way. However, later we will see that this form of organizing is most appropriate for charities that do not provide services which could lead to liability for the members of the organization.

Unincorporated organizations

Some unincorporated membership based organizations, such as local churches, are not organized on the basis of a Deed of Trust. These organizations are governed by what is commonly referred to as a Constitution and Bylaws. A distinction is sometimes made between an organization operating under a Deed of Trust and an organization operating under a Constitution and Bylaws. It is difficult to understand how such a distinction can be made in law. It is my understanding that an organization is either incorporated, and has some of the protection available in law because of the corporate veil shielding personal liability to the members, or it is not incorporated and personal liability flows through to the members of the organization.

One distinction which might be made between an unincorporated organization and a charitable trust is that of the accountability of the board members or trustees. Some lawyers claim that board members of both incorporated and unincorporated organizations are fiduciaries, but that the standards, duties, and obligations of trustees alone extend beyond those of a fiduciary. We will leave this issue for later consideration. However, at this point I will say that case law appears to be developing in the direction of deeming board members of charities to be like trustees, subject to the same standards, duties, and obligations of trustees.

An unincorporated charitable organization normally prepares a Constitution and Bylaws to govern its affairs. As stated earlier, I believe that bylaws are appropriate only for an incorporated organization. But, some government taxation authorities ask charities which are not incorporated, or which do not operate under a Deed of Trust, to submit their Constitution and Bylaws. Since this is the terminology used by some lawyers and certain government departments, I will use the same terminology in this discussion.

The constitution

The constitution part of the governing document basically describes the reason for the organization's existence, and the principles, or basis, on which the organization wishes to operate. It is very much like the declaration of trust section of a Deed of Trust. The bylaw portion of the Constitution and Bylaws regulates the internal practices and procedures of the organization. Bylaws define the rights and duties of the members, directors, and officers, along with how they relate to each other. The bylaws should be divided into articles that cover all the required areas.

The bylaws

There are generally two approaches that can be taken in drafting bylaws. The first approach is to have broadly written bylaws which embrace a general intent. This approach requires that a *Policy and Procedures Manual* be written to interpret the bylaws in exact detail. In this approach, the relationship between the bylaws and the policies and procedures is like the relationship between the legislation and the regulations which describe how the legislation is to be applied.

There are significant advantages with the broadly drafted approach. First, the bylaws will have a greater longevity. There is more likelihood that details need to be amended than that the broad intent of a bylaw becomes obsolete when circumstances change. Second, if changes in policies and procedures are required, the board of directors will be able to make the change without having to place the changes before the membership for approval.

Does this mean that a board can design the bylaws in such a way that they never have to go back to the members to change the bylaws? That would be unlikely. If changes in policies and procedures are so great that the letter, or intent, of the bylaws is altered, the bylaw itself must be changed. Most, but not all, bylaws require that a change in the bylaws must be presented to the membership for ratification.

It might seem to some, that assigning the power to change the bylaws to the governing board would be very efficient. But by assigning the power to amend bylaws to the governing board, the board may take on such a dominant role that the general membership no longer has any say in the development of the organization. Most organizations wish to retain a close relationship with their memberships so that the members will continue to support the organization's mission, and continue to contribute financially to the charity. It is often assumed that a healthy level of accountability to the membership fosters loyalty.

When you are dependent on a significant segment of the public for your donation income, donors should have the opportunity for a closer affinity with the organization. Members who know that they have the final say in any change in the direction, focus, and plans of the organization, probably, will feel a greater affinity and loyalty to the organization.

The lack of membership accountability can also occur when bylaws are written too broadly. In such a case, the board may have powers to change the focus and direction of the organization through changes to the policies and procedures manual, thereby effectively disenfranchising the members.

To avoid the possible abuses by interpreting broadly drafted bylaws by means of a policy and procedures manual, some membership organizations have opted to write detailed bylaws. This approach telescopes the policies and procedures manual and the broadly written bylaws.

The advantage of detailed bylaws is that the bylaws are quite specific. A change in the focus and direction of the organization must be approved by the membership. The disadvantage is that the board will frequently have to present bylaw changes to the membership. This may lead to much organizational time and effort being spent on internal organizational matters rather than fulfilling the organization's charitable mandate as stated in its objects. To be required to change bylaws frequently is very inefficient from an organizational objective point of view. Therefore, a membership organization which is dependent for its income on gifts from its membership needs to strike a delicate balance between efficiency and disenfranchisement.

Most common form of church organization

There is a full range of organizational structures among churches. However, based on my experience, I would conclude that most churches choose the unincorporated Constitution and Bylaws structure of organization. Many churches, especially those of the evangelical and independent variety, tend to avoid incorporation. The concern of those churches is that by incorporating they could become subject to state or government control.

Most mainline churches are incorporated. These churches usually are older, and some, like the Roman Catholic, Anglican, Lutheran and Episcopal churches have their roots in European countries where their "mother" churches were official state churches. There was no separation between church and state in the countries where many of these mainline churches had their origins. Consequently, such mainline churches have less fear of government interference and, therefore, usually opt for incorporation.

Incorporation

Incorporation is the most common form of organizing charities other than independent churches. This is primarily because members of incorporated charities are shielded from personal liability for actions, or lack of actions, taken by the corporation, or incorporated society. Later we will see that the corporate veil for directors of incorporated charities may be penetrated in many situations. But, members, who are not directors, are shielded from personal liability when an organization is incorporated.

The reason that the corporate veil is effective for the protection of the members of an incorporated charity, and not necessarily for the directors, is because directors of all corporations – both for-profit and not-for-profit, including charitable – are faced with a broad range of statutory and common law duties and responsibilities with which they must comply. For directors of charitable corporations, such obligations may be even broader than they are for directors of for-profit corporations. We will take a specific look at such issues in Chapter 5. At this time, we will look at the different forms of incorporation.

Incorporating as a society

Some jurisdictions have provisions for organizations to be incorporated as a society, while most states and provinces and the federal government require charities to incorporate under legislation designed primarily for profit-making corporations.

There is a difference between incorporating under society legislation and incorporating under corporate legislation. When a charitable organization is able to incorporate under legislation designed for non-profit organizations, the legislation is more likely to fit the unique nature of such an organization. There is less of a "fit" for an organization which must be incorporated under legislation which was designed primarily for the for-profit sector.

For instance, legislation designed for profit-making corporations deals extensively with the rights of the shareholders who are the real owners of the business. However, that same legislation is likely to be silent about the rights of the owners of charities. Remember the previous discussion that the real owner of charitable property is the public – not the members.

Take the issue of whether a director of an incorporated charity is a trustee as well as a fiduciary. If the legislation under which a charity must incorporate does not deal with the duties of directors of charities, the common law rules apply. But legislation designed for societies usually deals specifically, at least to some extent, with the powers and duties of directors. Such legislation designed specifically for the non-profit sector, usually, deals more realistically with the fiduciary duties to the public of a charity's directors.

Incorporating by means of special legislation

There is another method of incorporating besides incorporating under specific corporate or society legislation. Such method of incorporation is usually reserved for large national organizations, or in highly regulated fields, such as degree-granting institutions. In this situation, the organization may be required to incorporate by means of special legislation.

Directors of an organization incorporated by means of special legislation could be in a better position in relation to their fiduciary duties to the public. Unfortunately, such special legislation usually does not deal with the directors' fiduciary duties. The reason is that special legislative bills are drafted for specific purposes, like giving a university degree-granting powers. The drafters of such special legislation are concerned, primarily, with protecting the public from bogus or inappropriate degrees. Therefore, they concentrate their efforts on defining under which conditions, and by whom, degrees may be granted. When it comes to most other issues, the drafters of such special legislation include a clause to the effect that the legislation applicable to corporations applies in all areas not specifically dealt with in the legislative bill which establishes the special incorporation.

Special legislation for a university usually deals extensively with issues that affect the academic enterprise. I am not aware of any special legislation where the issues unique to board members of charities are dealt with by such legislation. That is unfortunate, because it leaves much confusion.

Let me give a specific example that applies in the province of Ontario. You will recall from the Introduction that the *Toronto Humane Society* case was decided in that jurisdiction. The issue in that case was whether directors may pay themselves salaries for serving the organization in any capacity.

Under most specific university legislation, the president is a member of the governing board. That makes the president a fiduciary and, possibly, a trustee of the university since a university is also a charity. Unless there is legislation specifically providing that board members may be remunerated for the services they provide to the university, there could be a breach of trust law when the board votes on the president's salary and benefits.

The special incorporation method of organizing as a charity is interesting. But, the opportunity to make use of that method is available to only a few organizations.

Articles of Incorporation or Letters Patent

To achieve incorporation in the usual manner, an organization applies for Articles of Incorporation, or Letters Patent, under the applicable federal, state or provincial legislation. The application document must be made in prescribed form and must contain prescribed information. This information, usually, must include the name of the corporation, the full address of the registered office, the number of directors, the names and addresses of the first directors, the objects under which the corporate charity may operate, and the powers it may exercise.

In some jurisdictions, this section of the Articles of Incorporation will be referred to an appropriate department in the attorney general's office, to determine if all the objects are charitable in law. The organizers should also review the relevant Revenue Canada and Internal Revenue Service publications, to ensure that the objects of the organization will pass the test to receive, or retain, charitable status or registration under income tax legislation.

In addition, the application will have to contain a statement that all the corporation's resources will be used exclusively for charitable purposes, and that the members and directors may not personally benefit from the charity. A statement as to how any remaining funds will be disbursed if the corporation is wound up, or dissolved, also must be included in this section.

This "winding up" provision is required by the taxation authorities to make sure that none of the property which was received by the charity will be used for non-charitable purposes. If this provision were not included in the governing document, the taxation authorities believe that some, or all, of the funds could be used for purposes for which tax exemption or tax credits, otherwise would not be available. This could happen because different jurisdictions may disagree as to which disbursements are charitable.

Previously, we discussed that there is some question as to where the dividing line exists between advocacy and education. As stated, "advancement of education" is charitable, but "advocacy" is not. Now let's assume that an organization obtains charitable status and is funded by a large single gift from a donor who receives a substantial deduction from taxable income, or substantial tax credits. After receiving the substantial gift, the charity could be wound up. The net assets of the charity could then be given to an organization which may be deemed to be a charity by a state or province, but which the taxation authorities had rejected for charitable status because some of the activities of the organization were thought to be "advocacy" rather than "education." Although the funds may be used exclusively for charitable purposes, the taxation authorities fear that they will loose the right to supervise the ultimate use of such funds if the transfer of such funds is not restricted to charities under their jurisdiction and control.

Consulting legal counsel

Going back to the application for incorporation process, some jurisdictions may require additional information. Since incorporation of a charity is a legal process which, hopefully, will be of benefit to the charity for many years, it is important that legal counsel be retained to draft both the application for incorporation, and any related documents.

Once the application has been reviewed, the registrar of corporations will issue a Certificate of Incorporation, or Letters Patent which incorporates all the information in the application into the final registered document. At that point, the charitable organization becomes a *person* in its own right, and a corporate veil is created between the members of the corporate person and the actions, or lack of actions, of the corporate person itself.

A newly incorporated charity should consult its legal counsel regarding the initial, and ongoing reporting requirements of the charitable corporation. Most lawyers, experienced with charities, will provide the charity with a reporting letter. This letter should provide the charity and its directors with all the information needed to ensure that the corporate status of the organization is properly maintained.

Corporate bylaws

Besides the Certificate of Incorporation or the Letters Patent, the new corporation also needs bylaws. The bylaws of a charitable corporation should contain all the elements discussed previously in relation to an unincorporated organization, with the addition of an article defining the use of the corporate seal. The considerations regarding broadly written, and highly detailed, bylaws, discussed previously, also apply to a charitable corporation.

Some jurisdictions require that the bylaws be submitted together with the application for incorporation. If such is the case, the bylaws are reviewed by the registrar to make sure that they meet the requirements of the governing legislation and current administrative practice. Other jurisdictions leave the authority of writing and amending bylaws exclusively to the corporation.

The fact that the bylaws must be submitted with the application for incorporation in some jurisdictions means that such jurisdictions take an interest in the contents of the bylaws. However, it does not mean that such interest relates specifically to the fiduciary duties of the directors of incorporated charities. If there are things in the bylaws which are objectionable under the legislation and current administrative policies, then they will have to be changed before the Certificate of Incorporation or the Letters Patent is issued. However, bylaw reviews by the registrar of corporations usually take place from the point of view of a for-profit corporation.

When the bylaws in some jurisdictions are reviewed during the incorporation process, can the charity obtain certain powers which otherwise could contravene trust law? For example, can a charity obtain the right to pay salaries to a director by writing such a provision into its bylaws when such is not allowed under common law?

The simple answer is no. Just because a government official reviews the contents of a document to make sure that it complies with the law, does not give that official the power to extend or change the law. If the specific legislation which governs registration of corporations does not provide for a certain power, the bylaws cannot be used to give the directors powers which are not allowed under common law.

Value and Mission Statement

Once the most appropriate organizational structure has been chosen or reviewed, the organization should write or review its value statement and mission statement. The public and the charity's supporters have a right to know which value sets underlie the organization's operations. In addition, a concise mission statement should communicate to all what activities the charity will undertake within the boundaries of the objects in the governing documents.

A clearly defined value statement and mission statement allow the public and the charity's donors to evaluate the effectiveness of the organization. It is part of the public accountability that should be required of all charitable organizations.

Summary of types of charitable organizations

A charity's form of organization – as a trust, an unincorporated society, or as a corporation – affects primarily the liability of the members and, to a lesser degree, the board of the organization.

Very little, if any, difference exists between an organization operating under a Deed of Trust and an unincorporated society operating under a Constitution and Bylaws. In both cases, the members of the charitable organization are personally exposed to liability for a wide range of actions that could be brought against the charity and its members.

In the case of an unincorporated charitable organization, organized by means of a Deed of Trust or a Constitution and Bylaws, the members are personally exposed to legal liability. We also saw that all members of a charity organized by means of a Deed of Trust are trustees when they exercise any direction or control over the property of the trust. As long as the powers of the members are restricted to electing new trustees, and receiving reports on the activities of the board, they likely will not be held responsible as trustees.

Some experts have argued that the charitable organization's Constitution and Bylaws define a trust between those who contribute property to the organization and those of the general public for whose benefit that property is used in accordance with the charitable objects.

If such is the case, the Constitution and Bylaws of an unincorporated society have the same status in law as a Deed of Trust. I am not aware of any court cases which can give some level of certainty in this matter.

Charities which raise funds primarily to support the charitable purposes of other charitable organizations are *not exposed* to the same potential liabilities as organizations which carry out their own charitable activities. This is simply because fundraising charities are exposed only to legal liability arising out of receiving donations, and the proper disbursement of donated funds to other tax-exempt, or registered charities.

Organizations which are actively involved in their own charitable activities, on the other hand, can be exposed to liabilities resulting from all their activities. This includes potential liability for the use of the organization's resources for other than the charitable purposes stated in the charity's objects. An example of such a use would be using the charity's funds for the advancement of religion when the objects of the organization do not allow for such expenditures.

Fundraising organizations, generally, are identified as charitable foundations. They usually include the word "foundation" in their name. Organizations carrying on activities in pursuit of their own charitable purposes, generally, are referred to as charitable organizations.

Both the *Income Tax Act, Canada* in Canada and the *Internal Revenue Code* in the United States of America make the distinction between charities which raise funds for other charities and those which perform their own charitable activities. Which classification will apply to a particular charity is determined by what a charity does; it is not determined by what words are included in the name of a charity.

There are charities which have the word "foundation" in their name, but which in reality perform their own charitable activities. Upon review, such a charity may be classified as a charitable organization. Therefore, inserting the word "foundation" in the name of the organization does not change its character.

For charities which are exclusively foundations, and for charities primarily active in disbursing grants and scholarships to individuals, it may be appropriate to be organized by means of a Deed of Trust. This method of organizing may also be an option for charitable organizations which have a very small membership base. In such a case, all members may be serving on the governing board of the charity and the protection for members is of little concern.

The benefit to the donor and the public may be the knowledge that trustees operating under a Deed of Trust are not attempting to shield themselves from personal liability. This may be viewed as an extra level of assurance that the trustees will apply the resources of the trust in accordance with the terms of the trust, and in accordance with the donor's instructions.

If trustees apply funds of a trust for purposes other than those specifically authorized in the deed of trust, the trustees will be required to replace such misapplied funds out of their own resources. The same will result if funds donated to a trust with a specific direction for their use are applied to another purpose, even if such other purpose is, itself, within the objects of the deed of trust.

When trustees are required to replace misapplied funds of the charity out of their own resources, they will not be entitled to receive a receipt to be used for income tax purposes. Such a replacement of misapplied funds is not a voluntary act. Therefore, such a forced transfer of funds would not be considered a gift in law. As noted above, to be recognized as a gift by the taxation authorities, a payment must be a "voluntary transfer of property, without valuable consideration."

In view of trust law relating to directors' and board members' duties and responsibilities to date, board members of charities would be wise to assume that they are trustees, and are to discharge their duties accordingly.

Questions for consideration

In light of the issues addressed in this chapter, members of the board should annually consider the following statements. By considering such issues, board members of charities will minimize legal liability for the organization, themselves and their members.

1. The board reviewed the activities of the charity over the past year in relation to the charitable objects in the governing document.

_____yes _____no

2. The board has a clearly defined, written value statement and mission statement which it communicates to all clients, the public, donors, and staff. ___yes ___no

3. The board has clearly defined the organization's plans and has determined that the plans are charitable and within the organization's objects. ___yes ___no

4. The board, at least every five years, reviews its objects and charitable purposes and takes action to ensure that strategic planning steps take place within the boundaries of the organization's existing or amended objects. ___yes ___no

5. The board, at least every five years, retains its legal counsel to review its objects and charitable purposes to ensure that its governing documents are appropriate for organization's activities. ___yes ___no

6. The board periodically reviews each program for its effectiveness and service to the public. ___yes ___no

THREE

Boards and Their Members

In the previous chapter, I said that membership-based charities should consider incorporating in order to shield their members from personal liability as well as the potentially high standards, duties, and obligations imposed by law on trustees. In this chapter, we will take a closer look at the issue of how the membership can retain a certain level of control over the organization without becoming trustees or fiduciaries.

Once the charitable organization has been formed as an unincorporated organization, or has obtained incorporation status, the bylaws need to be implemented. Included in the bylaws are the provisions for the nomination and election of the board members. The provisional board members of the organization, or their replacements, need to be elected in accordance with the bylaws to take office for the specified term.

Optimum size of a board

The governing documents normally state the number of board members required to serve the organization. Whether the number is prescribed by the governing documents or not, the issue of the optimum size of a board frequently comes up.

The most frequent question in relation to the size of a charity's board is whether there are too few members. Many charities in the United States of America, and Canada, have what has been called the "founder syndrome." The founder is usually a strong personality who has a clear vision as to what he, or she, wishes to accomplish through the charity. The founder does not like to be impeded in any way in his or her drive to achieve the organization's objectives. Therefore, the founder will frequently try to restrict the size of the board to the minimum number required by law. And even in such cases, the founder will hand-pick such board members.

At the other end of the board size spectrum is the national organization where all the chapters want equal say and influence in the decision making process. This is the parliamentary or representative type of organization. As a result, boards with forty or more members are not uncommon. The decision-making process and efficiency is usually significantly impeded in such large boards. This is even more so if the board members consider their allegiance and accountability to be primarily to the region or local constituency which appointed them to the national board. In such cases, it may take a number of board meetings before an issue can be decided.

Later we will discuss the results of such views in relation to the personal liabilities imposed on board members by specific legislation and common law. In the context of the current issue, only the effectiveness of a board's size needs to be considered.

The optimum board size is one which maintains a healthy balance between the efficiency and effectiveness of a board. A minimum number of board members are needed to have a representative range of skills involved in controlling and monitoring a charity, and to allow all board members the opportunity to participate in all deliberations. But when the size of a board exceeds a certain number, meaningful participation and contributions by all members becomes less likely.

There have been studies in the past to determine the optimum size of the board. There are many factors that need to be considered in such a study. No study can deal with *all* the variables. Therefore, no single number has come up. However, most of those who have considered the question of optimum board size conclude that a number of between nine and fifteen would appear to be appropriate. There are examples of efficient and effective boards where the number of board members is as low as three, and others where the number is substantially higher than fifteen. The most frequently quoted number is twelve. This may have its basis in the New Testament of the Bible where we find that Jesus selected twelve disciples. Since the religious sector is the largest in the charitable community, it is not surprising that this number has been identified as optimum.

Length of service

Another consideration to be made is the maximum length of time that a member should be allowed to serve on the board of a charity. Many organizations have a provision that directors may not serve for more than two consecutive three-year terms.

Why would an organization want to put that kind of a restriction on its directors? If a for-profit corporation has recruited a high-profile director who is able to make significant contributions to the company, the corporation will want to keep such a director as long as possible. Why would a charity take a different approach?

The automatic retirement provisions are usually incorporated into the bylaws to prevent an organization from becoming stagnant. In addition, they are designed to prevent the board members from perpetually reappointing themselves.

In a charitable organization, the board members have no form of personal ownership in the organization. Although that may also be the case with the outside directors in a public profit-making corporation, there are always enough directors who will be motivated because of their share-ownership to look after the best interests of the company and its shareholders. Such corporate directors know that their performance is ultimately measured by the return to the shareholders.

There is no such external accountability or method of evaluating the performance of a charity's board members. As a result, there is a much greater possibility for board members of a charity to become complacent. If such complacency becomes established in the board, the innovative and conscientious board members will likely resign. The remaining board members are more likely to appoint people who are their friends and turn the board into something like a "social club."

If the board becomes a social club, the board will no longer be motivated to look after the primary interest of the charity. The charity's board must pursue its charitable purposes in a most effective and efficient manner for the benefit of the public. In a situation where the board has become a social club, the organization is likely to lose its vitality and vibrancy.

Rotation of board members

Usually, the bylaws make provision for board members to be elected for terms which result in rotation. The purpose for such a provision is that not all board members will retire from the board at the same time. It is very important that there be continuity in the make-up of the board.

The proper rotation of board members is advisable, especially for charitable organizations which have a provision in their bylaws for automatic retirement of board members. For example, if a board consists of twelve members, one-third of the board positions should come up for re-election or retirement each year.

It is important that the re-election or retirement of board members be related to specific board positions, rather than persons. If the rotation is attached to persons, the rotation schedule can become so corrupted that the purpose for which rotation was primarily intended is negated. Let me illustrate this problem with an example.

Vacancies on the board of one charity caused by resignations resulted in the election of new board members. The retiring board members had resigned at various times during their three-year terms of office. The new board members were elected for full three year terms, not for the balance of the terms of the resigning board members. After a number of years of electing new board members in this manner, more than half of the board suddenly had to retire at the same time. The charity decided that it had to rectify this problem by electing new board members for shortened terms so that the original rotation schedule could be restored. It took three years before one-third of the board members could again be up for re-election or retirement each year.

The nominating process

Let's take a look at what I believe to be the best way to go about recruiting new board members to make sure that the charity remains vital and vibrant. In the past, it was generally viewed as an honour to be asked to serve as a director of a corporation, including a charitable organization. But now many people, who would make competent board members, are becoming aware of new legislation and the developing common law which imposes more and more duties and responsibilities on board members. As a result, the selection and recruitment process for a charity to secure quality board members has become both more difficult and important.

To achieve a proper mix of board members with the desired representation, qualities and expertise, most charitable organizations appoint a nominating committee.

Source of board nominees

A challenge faced by many charities is to develop a large enough membership pool from which new board members can be elected. I believe that every charity should have a membership which is distinct from the board. Those charities which are incorporated usually are subject to legislation which imposes a membership structure on them.

Under corporate legislation, the membership usually has the right to elect board members, to receive the financial statements, to receive the report on the financial statements prepared by the organization's external auditors, and to approve any changes to the organization's governing documents. Although these powers are frequently reserved for the members, there is a tendency in many organization to limit the number of members to those who are currently serving as board members.

An organization can develop a pool of qualified individuals by inviting those who have shown an interest in the organization's values and mission to become members. Such interest may have been expressed by means of volunteering time, or by donations made to the organization.

If an organization has a membership which is greater than the number of directors who currently serve on its board, the organization will have to make such membership meaningful. Besides the requirements of many statutes governing corporations, charities should provide the members with real involvement. At minimum, to give members a meaningful involvement, they should be involved in the nominating process. They should be entitled to approve the budgets as well as changes in the strategic plans of the organization. Without a meaningful involvement, members will soon lose interest in membership. Then it will be even more difficult to recruit new board members.

Taking membership involvement in an organization to the extreme can cause boards to be hampered from fulfilling their duties and responsibilities. In such extreme membership involvement situations, it is expected that members should be able to express themselves on too many issues. Care should be taken that the membership of a charitable organization understands that the board members are elected to be in charge of the charity. The membership cannot, and may not, interfere with those duties and responsibilities which are, by law, assigned to the board. However, if a proper balance between enfranchising the membership, and allowing the board to fulfill its duties and responsibilities can be found, a charity will be well served by its members. The membership can act as the "conscience" or "sounding board" for the public; nevertheless, only the board has the power to operate the charity.

Nominating committee members

Who should serve on the nominating committee? The problems of complacency and self-perpetuation could arise even when there is a provision for the rotation of directors, and even if a nominating committee is in place to recruit new board members. The nominating committee could nominate only those directors who retired the previous year, thereby frustrating the objective of recruiting new members to the board.

The provision for rotation and the establishment of a nominating committee do not in themselves guarantee that complacency and self-perpetuation problems will not develop. That's why I believe that nominating committees should be made up of a majority of members who are not currently board members, and who have not been board members for at least the past two years. Where a majority of the membership of the nominating committee is made up of those who have no vested interest in maintaining the status quo, there is a much greater potential for recruiting and electing new board members. Such new board members will likely come with new ideas, new energy and new enthusiasm for pursuing the charitable purposes of the organization.

Procedures of the nominating committee

As a first step, the nominating committee should prepare a list of potential candidates. The nominating committee may employ a specific process to arrive at its list of nominees. This process may include a discussion of the type of board member who needs to be elected.

For example, one issue to consider is whether the board's task is limited to policy development and monitoring, or whether it also includes implementation of the board's decisions in accordance with board policy. In the first instance, the board is a direction setting and policy making board. But, in the second case, the board also is a working board. When an organization is young, and has limited resources, the board is usually a working board. When the organization becomes more established and hires staff, it is more appropriate for the board to leave implementation of its policies to the staff.

The nominating committee may have to determine the primary selection criteria for new board recruits if these have not been defined in the committee's mandate. Selection criteria may include a consideration of representation. For example, it may be important that specific interest groups within the organization be represented on the board. Another selection criteria may be a specific set of skills that the new recruit is able to bring to the board. An example of a potential board recruit with specific skills may include a lawyer or an accountant. Other selection criteria may include such issues as program knowledge, gender, age, geographic location, political linkage, status, and a known ability to work with others as a member of a team.

In most jurisdictions, incorporated charitable organizations may select board members only from among their members. Also, a board member usually must be at least eighteen years of age, and not be an undischarged bankrupt.

Once the selection criteria have been established, the committee deliberates to see which of the members of the corporation or the community – currently not members or employees – meet the desired criteria. It is best to have a number of names for each criterion on the preliminary list.

When the preliminary list has been completed, each of the potential nominees needs to be assigned to a specific member of the committee, who will approach the prospect for a personal interview. The meeting with prospective board nominees should include a discussion regarding the background and plans of the organization, along with its accomplishments to date. The collective and individual roles of the board members should also be discussed. It should be made clear that, while the purpose of the meeting is to seek permission to place the individual's name in nomination, consent to do so does not guarantee that the prospect will be on the final slate, nor should being placed on the final slate be interpreted as an assurance of election. If the individual agrees to let his or her name stand for nomination, the committee member should request the potential nominee to provide relevant biographical information.

When all meetings with potential nominees have been completed, the nominating committee should meet to prepare a slate containing all eligible names and their biographical information for presentation to the board.

Nominating executive officers

Some organizations also ask the nominating committee to nominate those from among the members of the board who should be elected, or appointed, as executive officers of the board. In addition to a chairperson, the executive officers of a charity's board, at minimum, should include a secretary and a treasurer. Many charitable organizations also have one or more vice-chairpersons and a past-chairperson. The number of executive officers usually is a function of the organization's size and the size of its board.

It is my experience that the best way to assure a proper balance of new ideas and continuity among the executive officers – who normally also make up the executive committee – is to allow free elections by and from among the board members. Such elections to executive officer positions should take place at a meeting of the board right after the membership meeting.

Nominating committee report

In most cases, the board reserves for itself the final selection of names for presentation to the membership. But whether the board, or the nominating committee presents the nominees for board members to the membership, it is advisable to give the members a true choice in electing members to the board by presenting more than the number of names to be elected – preferably double the number to be elected. If the members are asked by the nominating committee, or the board, to cast their ballots for a slate of board members which is equal to the number of vacancies to be filled, the membership will soon get the message that their input is not really required. They will see themselves merely as "rubber stamps" to confirm the board's choices.

Summary of board and membership involvement

It is important for every charitable organization to have a vibrant and effective board. Charity boards should rotate their membership and see to it that new members can be recruited when needed. The best way to have a ready list of potential nominees for the board is to have a pool of members ready and willing to serve. To develop a pool of potential board members, such organization members need to fulfill meaningful functions. The right to vote on major organizational changes, to vote on major changes in the strategic plan, to participate on the nominating committee and to have true elections are but some of the ways in which organization members can experience true involvement.

Questions for consideration

To make sure that the organization remains vibrant and that it continues to serve a meaningful function, board members should evaluate their organization by answering the following questions. Questions answered in the negative may indicate that corrective actions may be required.

1. The organization does not allow members to serve on the board for more than six consecutive years. ___yes ___no

2. Does the board have a nominating committee to recruit new members and to nominate board members? ___yes ___no

3. Is the nominating committee made up of a majority of members who are neither current board members nor staff?
___yes ___no

4. Has the board adopted a written policy for the nominating committee to recruit new members and/or board members who possess the relationships, qualities and skills appropriate for the organization? ___yes ___no

5. Does the organization have a membership which is larger than the board? ___yes ___no

6. In your opinion, does the board have an appropriate number of board members with the required expertise for the organization's size? ___yes ___no

7. Does the board meet for at least three full agenda meetings per year? ___yes ___no

8. Is there rotation of board members so that a percentage of board members retire each year? ___yes ___no

9. Does the board have a formal education program for new board members either by orientation session and/or a reading program?
___yes ___no

FOUR

Powers of the Board and Conducting Meetings

This chapter will deal with the best way to conduct board meetings. I have had experience with a wide range of boards both in the for-profit and charitable sector. The most effective boards are those who establish a formal structure of procedures.

If a board does not have a clearly itemized agenda, it will be difficult to monitor how the meeting is progressing. Therefore, the chairperson should see to it that a clearly itemized agenda with supporting reports is presented to all board members in advance of each board meeting.

Powers and authority of board members

A charitable organization, whether incorporated or not, cannot act except through its agents. Board members individually are not the agents of the organization. Board members are the agents only when they act together as a board during a duly-called and constituted meeting. It is the board as a whole which has the power, duty, and responsibility to govern the corporation.

Where authorized by specific legislation, the board of directors of a corporation has the power to delegate certain powers and responsibilities to sub-agents – usually staff – who are not directors. However, there

are certain powers, duties, and responsibilities which a board cannot delegate, or assign to individuals, or groups, who are not board members.

A significant distinction between directors of for-profit corporations and board members of charitable organizations is that directors
of for-profit corporations may be remunerated for their services, while
board members of charitable organizations may not. Whether the
organization is incorporated or not does not make a difference.

Also, board members of charitable organizations may not be
employed by the organization of which they are board members,
unless they perform their services as volunteers. We briefly discussed
this issue in the Introduction and Chapter 1.

Powers of the chairperson

Some authorities and commentators take the position that the
chairperson of the board has powers which are greater than the powers of other board members. In some cases, I have seen bylaws which
give the chairperson enhanced powers.

It is my view that the unique functions of the chairperson are limited to chairing and setting the agenda for board meetings, for executive committee meetings (where such a committee exists), and for
membership meetings. In addition, the board as a whole may assign
specific tasks to the chairperson, as may be required from time to time.
However, such assignments should be task-specific with a requirement
to report back to the full board.

Later, when we deal with the duties and responsibilities of board
members (see Chapter 5), we will see that the legal liability to which
board members are exposed are not worth giving the chairperson special powers and authority. If a board decides to give such special powers to the chairperson, the board members will not be able to raise
such an action as a defence against personal liability. All board members remain personally liable for any acts or omissions that are a
responsibility of the board as a whole.

Delegating powers of the board

As stated earlier, the governing board of a charitable organization
has the responsibility, within the stated objects, to determine the poli-

cies of the organization, and to see to it that those policies are implemented. This includes determining the areas of activity in relation to available and potential resources, and the scope and development within each of those areas. When implementing activities in each of the selected areas, the board may act for itself by volunteering its services, or it may select and supervise staff.

If the governing board implements its activities through staff, the board has the responsibility to monitor the staff's performance through reviewing reports and financial statements prepared by the staff, and through various standing committees, such as the executive committee and the audit committee.

Making sure that board policies and decisions are implemented properly

The only way to make sure that all board actions are taken in a correct and precise manner, is to have all board decisions recorded in precise resolutions in the minutes of the board. In addition, the process of arriving at such decisions is important. Every board member should be informed of the procedures to be followed when bringing matters to the attention of the board, and how the board will deal with such matters. For this reason, it is important that the board establish rules of order for its conduct as well as for the conduct of its committees.

The governing board of a charity should have rules of order which deal with specific procedures not covered in the bylaws. If the organization has adopted highly detailed bylaws, some, or all, procedures at board meetings may already be included in that document. However, in the majority of charities that will not be the case.

Rules of order

The scope of the rules of order depends to a large extent on the size of the organization. The larger the organization is, the more detailed its rules of order should be.

For example, let's assume that an organization which is the size of the relief and development organization where John was elected to the board (see the Introduction). The board of that organization must conduct its affairs by means of highly structured rules which will deal with a number, if not all, of the issues which I have listed below.

Sample Rules of Order

1. In the absence of both the chair and the vice-chair, the CEO will call the meeting to order; a member of the board will then be designated to preside at such a meeting.

2. If the chair, the vice-chair, and the CEO are all absent at the time for opening the meeting, but a quorum is present, the board members present will designate a chair from among themselves to direct the discussions of the meetings.

3. The chair of the board, or of a board committee, may express an opinion on any subject under debate, but before doing so, the chair shall appoint the vice-chair, or, in his or her absence, another member, to take the chair until a final decision on the question has been taken.

4. Any member who desires to speak, shall address the chair, who shall recognize the member. The member may then, but not before, proceed to address the meeting. When two or more members simultaneously ask the chair to address the meeting, the chair will determine the order in which the members are to speak.

5. A member addressing the chair will be interrupted only by another member who wishes to raise a point of order, or of privilege. That member must then restrict his or her comments to the point raised.

6. A member may speak no more than three times, and not longer than fifteen minutes in total on the item under discussion, unless permission of the meeting is granted. The mover of a motion will be allowed an additional three minutes to reply to issues raised on the motion.

7. A member may, at any time during the debate of a motion, request that the motion be read; but such a reading will not have the effect of interrupting the speaker.

8. A member may demand that notice be given at the meeting before a new motion is placed before the board. If most of the

members present vote in favour of such a demand, the motion will then be introduced at the next meeting.

9. Every motion and amendment, except a motion to adjourn, must be made and seconded before the chair can place it in debate, and before it becomes part of the record. Unless the mover is allowed to withdraw the motion, it can be disposed of only by a vote of the majority of members present.

10. No member introducing a motion, may speak to the issue until the motion has been read by the chair.

11. Any member who has given a notice to introduce a motion, may withdraw such notice with the consent of the majority of members present.

12. When a motion is under debate, no other motion will be received, except a motion,

    1. to amend.

    2. to adjourn the debate (table),

    3. for the previous question (in case of an amendment),

    4. to lay on the table, (i.e. to discuss a previously tabled motion),

    5. to postpone the discussion (table temporarily), or

    6. to refer to committee.

13. A motion to adjourn the debate, or for the previous question, or to lay on the table will be voted on without debate.

14. A motion to adjourn the debate is always in order, but no second motion having the same effect will be made until some other business intervenes.

15. A motion to refer a matter to committee until it is decided upon will preclude all amendments to the main motion.

16. A motion for the previous question to be called, may be moved at any time when a motion, or an amendment, is before the chair. When the motion for the previous question is moved, the chair will allow all those who have previously asked for the floor to speak before stating the question: "Are we ready for the question?" If the question is answered in the affirmative, the chair will

immediately place the question for the motion and amendments, then before the chair, in the reverse order in which they have been moved. Such motions will then be voted on without further debate.

17. All amendments will be called in the reverse order in which they have been moved, except filling blanks relating to time and amounts, when the longest time and the largest amount will be called first. Every amendment submitted will be decided upon, or withdrawn, before the main motion is put to a vote.

18. Only two amendments, i.e. an amendment and an amendment to an amendment, can be proposed at the same time. When one or more have been disposed, a further amendment or amendment to an amendment may be entertained by the chair.

19. When the motion under debate contains several propositions or issues, upon the request of any member, the motion may be split. In such a case a vote will take place on each of the parts.

20. No member shall speak to a motion after it has been called by the chair, nor shall any other motion be made until after the result is declared. The decision of the chair as to whether a question has been called shall be conclusive.

21. When the chair has to decide a point of order or practice, the chair, if requested to do so, will state the rule applicable to the case without argument, or comment. When calling for the question, the chair will observe the order in which the motions were presented.

22. A member being called to order will have the opportunity to explain.

23. A ruling of the chair will be subject to an appeal to the meeting without debate.

24. The request of one-third of the members present for permission to present a motion for reconsideration at the same meeting or at a subsequent meeting will be granted. But to obtain the approval for such a reconsideration, the motion must receive the support of a majority of the members present.

25. A motion to reconsider will not be reconsidered again once it has been defeated.

26. When a special committee is appointed, the board shall designate the chair and the secretary.

27. All questions, petitions, enquiries, or communications, which the chair decides should be sent to committee, will be referred by the chair to the appropriate committee without any motion. Unless a majority of the members present determine that the question should not be dealt with by the committee receiving the matter, the committee shall make recommendation on the matter to the chair.

28. The rules and practices of parliamentary procedure not inconsistent with these rules will govern the board, and all committees, in all applicable cases.

29. Upon the vote of the majority of the members present and voting, any rule, or part thereof, may be suspended, or adjourned, for any meeting. The rule, or part thereof, to be suspended, or adjourned, must be stated clearly and succinctly.

30. In the event of a personal attack, the chair of the meeting will call the offender to order immediately, making it clear that such behaviour cannot be tolerated.

31. The chair should immediately, and publicly disassociate the rest of the committee, or board, from personal attacks that may be made by one member upon another.

32. Reports for presentation by board committees to the board will be presented by the chair of such committees, or by his or her designated substitute.

The board acting through committees

Previously, it was stated that a board of directors may act through committees appointed for such purposes. At this time, we will take a closer look at how to go about such assignments and restrictions that may apply.

There are few restrictions as to when a board may assign a responsibility to a committee, except that the board may not delegate responsibilities which it must, by law, perform itself. As long as the board is aware that actions which it has delegated to a committee remain the responsibility of the board as a whole, there is nothing against delegating specific tasks, or responsibilities, to committees. Actually, there is very little, if any, difference between delegating responsibilities to committees and delegating them to management. In general, when the bylaws permit, and the law allows, the governing board may perform certain of its responsibilities by means of committees.

For example, many governing boards of charitable organizations elect an executive committee from among their members. Such an executive committee is normally assigned all the powers of the board between the meetings of the board. The board usually requires the executive committee to report its actions to the next meeting of the board.

The board has the power to confirm, modify, or rescind the decisions of the executive committee. However, the board does not have the power to reverse actions when a third party has acted on the decisions of the executive committee in good faith. If the board believes that it is forced to reverse the action of the executive committee in such situations, the organization will be liable for any losses incurred by the third party. The extent of such losses could include the loss of profit.

Subject to the bylaws, the governing board at all times retains the power to expand, or restrict the powers of the executive committee; but only to the extent that the board itself has power to act.

The audit committee

The audit committee is one of the most important committees that a charity board should appoint to protect its fiduciary responsibilities. The purpose of the committee is to meet with the external auditor at least twice each year.

During the first meeting between the audit committee and the external auditor, the scope and focus of the upcoming audit should be discussed. At this time, the committee has opportunity to enquire of the auditor whether there are any concerns the auditor wishes to address as a result of observances during previous audits. The committee also has opportunity to draw to the attention of the auditor special areas which it would like reviewed in more detail than might have been planned by the auditor.

The second meeting of the audit committee with the external auditor is to review the audited financial statements along with the audit findings. The management letter, or audit comments, prepared by the auditor are usually reviewed during this meeting. During the second meeting, the audit committee also discusses the auditor's willingness to continue to serve as auditor of the organization. At this meeting, the auditor's remuneration for the next year is also discussed.

The audit committee reports all its findings and recommendations to the board of directors.

Members of the audit committee

There has been some debate regarding the need for an audit committee made up exclusively of members of the governing board. The question has been asked whether it wouldn't be more beneficial for the organization to have financial experts, who are not board members, on such a committee. This question usually arises where there is a lack of understanding of the purpose for the audit committee.

The purpose for an audit committee must not be confused with the function and task of an internal audit group, or a finance committee of an organization – usually made up of, or at least including employees. The purpose of the audit committee is to be a direct link between the external auditor and the full board, without interference by management. In this way, the board discharges its duty to examine the organization's books first-hand – not through the eyes of management. This duty is precisely the type which the board may not delegate to non-board members.

Requirement to appoint an executive committee and an audit committee

There is no requirement to appoint an executive committee or an audit committee. Especially in smaller organizations, the full board may decide to perform all the functions that may be performed by an executive committee or an audit committee. But, it should be stressed that the board cannot delegate its responsibilities for the external audit to employees or non-board members.

Other committees

In addition to the executive and audit committees, the governing board may appoint such other committees as the bylaws allow. Such committees may be standing or *ad hoc*.

If the board gives a committee a mandate which by statute, or the organization's bylaws, covers powers reserved for the governing board, the board must appoint only board members to such a committee.

Other committees may be augmented by such non-board members as may serve the purpose of the board, or the committee. It should be remembered that the governing board, or a committee, provided the board approves, may invite non-board members to serve as resource persons to any committee, including the executive and audit committees.

Legal role and task of each board member

The courts, in some cases, have characterized directors of for-profit corporations as both agents and trustees. The directors of a for-profit corporation have duties, and owe allegiance to all the stakeholders of the corporation, including the shareholders, employees, fellow directors, creditors, and the public at large. Such duties and allegiances are expanded for charitable organizations to include donors, and instead of shareholders, the public is the primary stakeholder of charitable organizations.

As discussed previously, members of a board have powers only when they act at meetings of the board. Other than at official meetings of the board, members of the governing board have no powers, except those specifically assigned by resolution of the board. Such restrictions apply to board members of for-profit as well as charitable organizations – whether incorporated or not.

Board members as trustees of a charitable organization

There is a significant body of case law which characterizes a charitable organization as a trustee which holds its assets in trust for use in implementing its charitable purposes. This body of cases extends the trustee analogy to the board members. An organization is not able to act on its own behalf; it must act through its agents – the board members. It is reasoned that board members occupy a position of trust toward all the stakeholders of the charitable organization. They must act in good faith toward all these stakeholders, i.e., they may not favour one to the detriment of the others.

Whether board members of charitable organizations, other than those operating as a charitable trust, are trustees, in the strict legal sense of that word, remains to be determined. The judge in the, now famous, *Toronto Humane Society* case, where the controlling board members of the Society had paid themselves salaries out of the charity's funds for services rendered as its officers, decided that a charitable organization is answerable for the use of its property as though it were a trustee. The judge's reasoning was based on earlier decisions that board members are fiduciaries and, as such, are not allowed to make a profit from their offices. They cannot allow themselves to be placed in a position where their interests and duties conflict with those of the public.

Let me quote a paragraph from the *Toronto Humane Society* case. The judge said,

> "Whether one calls them trustees in the pure sense (and it would be a blessing if for a moment one could get away from the problems of terminology), the directors are undoubtedly under a fiduciary obligation to the society and the society is dealing with funds solicited or otherwise obtained from the public for charitable purposes. If such persons are to pay themselves, it seems to me only proper that it should be upon the terms upon which alone a trustee can obtain remuneration, either by express provision in the trust document or by the order of the court."

Whether board members of charitable organizations are trustees in law, appears to be important only in determining how far liability for negligence extends. As noted earlier, trustees must act together as a unit. This means that a trustee cannot rely on the defence which may be available to a fiduciary, that they were not aware of the actions of the remaining trustees. All trustees are required to properly supervise the actions of fellow trustees.

Until the courts resolve the issue of trusteeship definitively, it seems prudent for board members of charitable organizations to assume that they may be judged to be trustees in the full meaning of that word. As such, it would be prudent for board members to attend all board meetings. It also would be prudent to insist that the board pass a resolution that all decisions of the board dealing with the assets of the organization must be made only when all members of the board are either present, or when they have received proper notification of the proposed action.

If decisions of the governing board are made by the members acting together, both honestly, and in good faith, there is a statutory provision in most jurisdictions enabling the courts to excuse the board members if they have breached a trust, or if a loss occurred.

Board members as agents of the charitable organization

Board members of the organization are agents only when acting in the name of, and on behalf of, the organization, provided they act within their actual authority. If board members while acting on behalf of the organization, inform a third party that they are acting with board authority, and if the third party has reason to believe that the board members have authority to act on behalf of the organization, then the third party may accept that the board members are acting as agents for the organization.

If it is subsequently discovered that the board members did not have authority to act, the organization is still liable to the third party, but the organization may sue the offending board members for unauthorized costs incurred. Board members may act only within the authority given by means of a board resolution. This means that board members may bind the organization in a commercial transaction only if the board has passed a resolution giving such board members the power to bind the organization. Many legal documents which are to be signed by board members will have the phrase "I have authority to bind the organization" printed below the signature line. The inclusion of this phrase gives comfort to the other party because the other party may rely on such a signed statement, unless the other party has reason to believe that the statement is false.

Ordinary agency law applies to board members of charitable organizations. As a result, a board member, who does not carry out the resolution of the governing board, which he or she has agreed to carry out, is liable for any loss to the charitable organization resulting from the board member failing to carry out the resolution.

On the other hand, a board member who acts on behalf of the charitable organization in good faith, may be entitled to indemnification from the organization, provided the charitable organization has the power for indemnification within its bylaws, and further provided that it has the legal authority to offer such indemnification in its home state or province.

The greatest potential for liability for the unwary board member of a charitable organization is a failure to understand that a board member only has limited authority – authority which is limited by the decision of the governing board acting as a whole.

The duties and obligations of board members of charitable organizations are derived in part from trust law, and in part from agency law. Board members are trustees of the organization's money and property, and agents in relation to the transactions they enter into on behalf of the organization.

Board members of charitable organizations are at least fiduciaries. As fiduciaries, they are subject to the same duty of loyalty as trustees. They are required to meet the standard of care defined in law. As agents, board members of charitable organizations have authority limited by the bylaws and resolutions of the governing board. Each board member must act within those limits.

Board members of charitable organizations should annually review the following statements. The purpose of such a review is to determine the extent to which they accurately apply to the organization and all of its individual board members.

Questions for consideration

Answers to the following questions and statements will assist board members to determine if they are discharging their responsibilities in a way that limits their exposure to liability.

1. Is a written agenda with supporting documents sent to each board member at least ten days prior to each board meeting?

    ___yes ___no

2. Are meetings conducted in accordance with written rules of order?   ___yes ___no

3. Are all board committee minutes sent to all board members and reviewed at the next following board meeting?   ___yes ___no

4. Are all board minutes recording motions, including any required actions, approved and signed at the next following board meeting and kept in the official records of the organization?

    ___yes ___no

5. Is all information necessary for board members to make informed decisions, and to make it possible for each board member to discharge his or her legal duties, being shared with all board members without exception?   ___yes ___no

6. Does the board consult professional experts (e.g. lawyers and accountants) when issues arise which require special expertise?

    ___yes ___no

7. The board chairperson does not have special powers, other than chairing meetings and setting agendas for meetings.

    ___yes ___no

8. Does the organization have an audit committee of at least 3 persons?   ___yes ___no

9. Is the audit committee made up exclusively of board members?

    ___yes ___no

10. Does the board have each board member annually evaluate his or her participation at board meetings?   ___yes ___no

FIVE

Duties of Board Members

In a number of previous chapters, I have stated that board members of charities, at minimum, have fiduciary duties. In addition, I have stated that there is a body of court cases which appears to impose the responsibilities of trustees on board members of charities as well. At this time, we will take a closer look at the legal duties of charity board members.

There are a number of specific duties which are imposed on board members of charities. These duties are as follows: *the duty of honesty, the duty of loyalty, the duty of care, the duty of diligence, the duty of skill, and the duty of prudence.* I will deal with each of these duties in some detail. However, you should be aware that the commentary under each duty has been developed by considering court cases, and commentaries on such cases, which relate primarily to for-profit corporations.

The duty of honesty

Every board member of a charity must act with honesty, in good faith, and in the best interest of the organization. In their dealings with fellow members, board members must tell the whole truth. Board members can be held personally liable for the misuse of the organization's funds, or the misappropriation of funds.

The duty of honesty includes the requirement to share with all the board members any knowledge of illegal or improper acts of employees. If a board member has such knowledge, and does not share it with all the board members, the board member can also be held liable for such acts if they result in material loss to the charity.

A board member may not act fraudulently. He or she must be open and candid about dealings which affect the organization. This duty of dealing honestly also extends to the requirement to see to it that all transactions, or decisions, are within those authorized by the organization's incorporating statute or other governing document.

Included in the duty of honesty and loyalty (discussed below) is the requirement to exercise confidentiality in matters presented to the governing board. Breaching the obligation of confidentiality, while it may not attract any specific legal liability, is inconsistent with dealing in the best interest of the organization. Therefore, a board member should not be permitted, either during, or after the term of office, to use confidential information obtained in the capacity as a board member for personal or other use. The best way to assure confidentiality would be to have every board member sign a statement of confidentiality and non-disclosure when the board member is first appointed or elected.

The duty of loyalty

Because board members are fiduciaries, they are subject to the common law of loyalty. This duty requires board members to act honestly, and to avoid any conflict of interest between themselves and the charitable organization.

Board members of charitable organizations must meet the general standards of loyalty and good faith. They must avoid any conflict of interest between their own self-interest and the interests of the organization. In other words, a board member of a charitable organization must work exclusively in the interest of the organization, and avoid all conflict of interest which may result in direct or indirect personal profit.

The courts have taken the position that no fiduciary can have an interest that conflicts with the interests of the organization's beneficiaries, or the public, whom each board member is obligated to protect. The fact that an offending transaction may have been fair and reasonable is neither an excuse, nor a defence, in conflict of interest situations.

In the strict view applied in some court cases, it has been suggested that the test of liability is simply whether a board member has, or can have, a personal conflict. Consequently, a board member may be liable for any personal profit made. If, while the board member was in a fiduciary capacity, the board member has made a profit as a result of being in that fiduciary relationship, personal liability may result.

There is no general rule as to when legal action can, or should, be taken against an offending board member by a governing board of a charitable organization, when such a board member personally profited from a conflict of interest. There is also no certainty as to the potential liability board members of a charity may incur if they depart from acting exclusively in the best interests of the charity.

Even if the charity is not in a position to take advantage of an opportunity, the board member, as a fiduciary, may not be able to introduce such a fact as a defence, if he or she is charged with a conflict of interest. It would appear to be prudent for board members to anticipate legal liability where a conflict exists. Legal liability can occur even when the charity is not in a position to take advantage of the opportunity and, therefore, no loss will be suffered by the charity.

A board member, at all times, is exposed to the liability of the standard of loyalty to the organization. The board member may be required to give account of all his or her actions to the board of the organization. In addition, accountability may be required to the public at large as well as to government regulatory bodies. As such, board members of a charity have the responsibility to ensure that all the charity's resources are used exclusively for charitable purposes. In addition, they must be satisfied that no part of the income can be used for the personal benefit of any of the board members, or of any members of the organization.

It should be noted that the duty of loyalty may continue even after the person is no longer a member of the governing board of the organization. Therefore, to simply resign from the board, when a conflict of interest situation arises, is not sufficient. A case in point would be a situation where it could be shown that the board member resigned in order to benefit from a transaction that would have resulted in a conflict of interest, had the board member not resigned.

The duty of care

The duty of care requires a board member of a charity to act with prudence and diligence. Prudence, in this context, means that the duty of care is based on common sense, not on experience (as in the case of the duty of skill).

In a sense, the duty of care combines all of the duties and states that a board member must show honesty, loyalty, and diligence. But the board members does not need to show any skill beyond ordinary common sense and the experience actually acquired. Therefore, the duty of care may vary to some extent, depending on the background and experience of each individual board member.

The requirement to act with diligence, in the context of the duty of care, means that the board members must keep themselves informed about the policies, activities, and affairs of the organization. Such fiduciaries must be aware of the tasks and activities of the officers. They must also have general knowledge about how the charitable activities of the organization are carried out; how the organization derives its revenue; and how the resources are used for the charitable purposes of the organization.

As an example of how the courts are developing the duty of care, a Delaware case is instructive. In 1994, Caremark International, Inc. pleaded guilty to violating United States of America health care laws. As a result of the plea, the company had to pay substantial fines and civil damages. These fines and civil damages resulted in a substantial decline in share value. As a result, shareholder claims were filed against the directors claiming that they had breached their fiduciary duty of care. The argument was that the directors had failed to monitor the activities of the company's management *or to put in place measures that may have prevented the unlawful conduct.*

When this case was finally settled late in 1996, the court said that a director's duty of care includes "a duty to attempt in good faith to assure that a corporate information and reporting system, which the

Board concludes is adequate, exists." In this particular case, the court decided that the company did have "adequate" information and reporting systems in place. The test of adequacy, the court said, is to determine whether such a system is reasonably designed to provide the board with timely, accurate information so that the board can "reach informed judgments concerning both the corporation's compliance with the law and its business performance."

The positive side of this decision is that it may provide boards with a defence in the future. Assuming that a board has implemented an "adequate" and effective information and compliance system, the exposure of board members for liability may be reduced.

The duty of diligence

A board member of a charity is required to make such enquiries on activities and proposals which a person of ordinary care, in that person's position, would make in relation to the management of his or her own affairs. Therefore, a board member is at all times required to remain informed about the policies, activities, and affairs of the organization. Failure to pay attention to these diligence requirements could be interpreted as an indication of dishonesty. If a board member fails to perform some act which that board member was responsible to perform, such neglect may be construed as a breach of the duty of diligence.

If a board member suspects that some board members are privy to information, relating to the governance and management of the charity, which have not been shared with all other board members, then such a board member has the duty to see to it that no secrets are kept from any of the other board members. If such a board member fails to make sure that the information is shared with all the board members he, or she, could also be accused of lack of due diligence.

On the other hand, if a board member suspects that he or she is not receiving all the information required to discharge his or her responsibilities as a member of the board, that board member should resign. The board member who resigns should deliver a written reason, either in person, or by registered mail, to the organization. The potential liability voluntarily accepted by a board member of a charity is not worth the risk, if all board members do not deal openly and in good faith with one another.

The duty of skill

Like the duty of care, the duty of skill requires prudence. Because of this, the duties overlap to a certain extent. However, the types of prudence required for the two duties are different. The duty of care requires prudence based on common sense, whereas the duty of skill requires prudence based on experience.

Under common law, a board member is not expected to exercise any skill which the board member does not have. The board member is not expected to be an expert unless appointed because he or she possesses a specific set of skills. If the board member is an expert in any field, he or she must use that knowledge for the organization's benefit. Obviously, the degree of skill required differs with the qualifications of the board member.

Finally, it should be noted that under common law, board members will not be liable for mere errors in judgement. But, it should also be noted that the common law duty of skill has been expanded, in recent legislation, for directors of profit-making corporations in many jurisdictions.

In view of the change in the requirement for skill in the for-profit sector over the last number of years, it would appear prudent for charitable organizations to assume that similar requirements for skill will be applied to their board members. This approach would appear to be prudent even for charities which are located in jurisdictions that do not have unique legislation for the not-for-profit sector. To determine whether a board member has passed the test of skill, future courts may give consideration to the following factors:

1. the qualifications of the board member,
2. the significance of the action,
3. the information available to the board member,
4. the time available for making the decision,
5. the alternatives open to the board member,

6. whether the board member is a representative of a special interest group (government, clients, community), and

7. whether the board member is an advisor to the organization (lawyer, accountant, engineer).

The duty of prudence

The duty of prudence requires board members to use common sense, and to act carefully, deliberately, and cautiously in trying to foresee the likely consequences of a proposed course of action.

The common law does not make board members liable for honest mistakes. Board members are not required to go beyond the limits of their own knowledge and ability when they consider the prudence of a particular course of action. However, corporate law has been moving to a more restrictive requirement for a corporate director to show prudence. The newer test, which may also be applied to board members of charities in the future, requires a director to meet the standard of the "reasonably prudent person." This requirement may make it necessary for a board member to be educated, to a level sufficiently advanced, to be able to understand a proposal before a decision is made.

Board member responsibilities as a result of their duties

Earlier, I reviewed the duties of board members as they are applied primarily in the for-profit sector. As a result of those duties which are, or could be, imposed on board members of a charity, all board members should consider their actions, or lack of actions, in light of such duties. At this point, I will consider some specific situations which have happened in the charitable sector.

One way in which charity boards frequently fail to discharge their legal duties is by "following the leader." A charity may become aware of a certain set of facts and take the opportunity presented by such facts to the board. The board frequently limits its enquiry regarding the proposed action to determining which other charities have taken the proposed course of action. One example of the "following the leader" syndrome was the Foundation for New Era Philanthropy which operated in the United States of America in the mid 1990s.

The Foundation had offered major charities in the United States an opportunity to double any eligible money deposited with the Foundation. The Foundation had claimed that it had anonymous, wealthy donors who were prepared to help worthy causes by doubling such charities' funds which were newly raised and which were not needed for current operating purposes. To prove that the charity had eligible funds, the charity was required to deposit such new funds with the Foundation for a period of six months. The controlling director of the Foundation appeared to be a well-connected and respected person.

The first charities to take the risk found that double their original funds were returned to them after six months as promised. This result was published and went through the charitable community like wildfire. Many charities became interested in this new source of cash. Most of those charities, which became interested in the Foundation, did no further diligence checks than to read the success reports by charities which had already experienced the windfall. The new participating charities did not want to be left out, and wanted to get their share of gifts from the anonymous, but wealthy philanthropists. They wanted to participate before the funds ran out.

It turned out that the Foundation was operating nothing more than a sophisticated Ponze Scheme. There were no wealthy philanthropists supporting the Foundation's money doubling program. The Foundation was able to pay out the doubled funds to the first depositors because the funds from new depositors were used to make the payments. As long as incoming funds exceeded double the payout, the Foundation was able to keep up the scam. But this scheme was destined to collapse.

As noted, many highly respected charities became victims of this scam. Thankfully, the charitable sector came together after the scam was exposed, and took action to avert the normal serious consequences of such scams. The actions these charities took is a testament to charity. The charities which had been the "beneficiaries" of doubling their funds, agreed to return the excess funds to a trustee so that he could redistribute such funds to those charities which were faced with large losses. After everything was settled, the net losses were minuscule compared to what they could have been.

The purpose of recounting the story here is not to open wounds for those affected by the scam. Neither is it my intent to point fingers at those who were taken in by the scheme. Major respected charities had been taken in by the scam because it was so believable and exciting to them. Well known and respected names had been used in perpetrating the fraud. However, in hindsight, there were some troubling signs which indicated that all might not be as good as it appeared. The purpose of recounting this story here is to help board members to identify early warning signs. Four major concerns were:

1. If something sounds too good to be true, it usually is. In hindsight, it might be easy to make this statement. However, the Foundation should have been able to show independently audited financial reports to prove that the matching funds were available. The Foundation was never able to produce audited financial statements, let alone statements which showed sufficient reserve funds to back up its scheme.

2. Charities were asked to deposit their newly raised funds with the Foundation. This was supposed to be a "good faith" act by the charities to prove that the funds were not needed for current operations. In hindsight, it is easy to state that there are better and more sound ways to determine whether a charity has funds eligible for matching grants. A signed statement by the charity's independent auditor would have been more meaningful. After all, a charity could have taken an amount out of its normal operating funds and used borrowed funds over the six month period for operations. The requirement to deposit the funds with the Foundation was non-negotiable, but it was also the least believable of the requirements. A number of the charities recognized this weakness and insisted that the deposit be placed with an independent third party. The Foundation agreed to this demand in some cases, but found a way to make use of the deposited funds in any case. The fraud was perpetrated at a number of levels and a major investment firm experienced a substantial loss as a result.

3. Charities should always ask the question whether they can make the proposed "investment" to achieve the gain. The deposits with the Foundation were not the type of investment which would be considered prudent from the point of view of trust law. A charity holds all funds in trust for its charitable purposes. If a charity has surplus funds, it must invest such funds in investments approved for trustees in the charity's legal jurisdiction. New Era did not pay interest on the "invested" funds. As a matter of fact, they were interest-free, term deposits. The matching funds were not a return on investment, but rather a reward from a third party for having met the matching requirement. Therefore, the "investments" themselves were not acceptable under trust law. A no-interest investment is not in the best interest of the charity or its intended beneficiaries.

4. Many of the charities relied on the positive reports from other respected charities. To be able to discharge their fiduciary duties, boards of charities must do their own due diligence. As we have seen above, it is not a defence to be able to state that reliance was placed on the actions or statements of others, unless it can be shown that such reports, themselves, would meet the test of due diligence. Following the leader can bring those that follow into serious difficulty.

The charitable sector is constantly being exposed to new scams. In my work with the Canadian Council of Christian Charities, I see a number of new ones every year. There is one common theme in all of them. The common theme is that there is something secretive about each one. Some key aspect of the opportunity either cannot be disclosed until the charity has signed a non-disclosure and non-competition agreement, or it is cloaked in some other form of anonymity. In addition, such scams usually require some kind of fee or deposit, before the source of the benefits can be revealed or sent to the charity. Be very wary of secret wealth. Before responding to any "miraculous" offer, refer the material to your professional advisors. It may sound ungrateful to look a "gift horse in the mouth," but it is the prudent thing to do.

Election or appointment of board members by special interest groups

There are situations in some charitable organizations where some board members are appointed, or elected, by a specific group, or umbrella organization. This frequently happens in denominationally controlled organizations. It also happens in organizations which have a presence in more than one country. The "parent" organization attempts to control the local organization by exercising direction and control over the board of the "subordinate" charity.

The tendency in such situations is that the board member appointed, or elected, in that way sees him or herself as representing the appointing group or organization. Such a view is in conflict with the board member's fiduciary duty to act in the best interest of the organization which the person serves as a board member.

A board member must always act with independence of mind, and operate exclusively in the best interest of the organization he or she is serving as a board member. This means that he or she cannot be influenced by outside bodies.

Contracting with other board members or bodies

For this same reason, a board member cannot contract, either with another board member, or with an another body, as to how the member will vote at a meeting of the board. A board member's duty and responsibility is always to the organization and not to the body which appointed or elected the member.

Attending meetings

A member of the governing board is not required to attend all the meetings of the board. But, the member should attend as often as possible. If a board member fails to attend board meetings on a reasonably regular basis, the board member may be held liable for decisions about which the member had no knowledge.

Although failure to attend meetings is not, in itself, a liability, it may be evidence of a lack of diligence. However if the board member is not able to attend a meeting, he or she could show diligence by examining the minutes of the meetings which were missed as well as by talking with other officers and directors about those meetings. Where a member can show that such independent actions were taken, the member probably would have shown sufficient diligence to escape liability.

Agreement with actions of the board

When a member of the governing board is present at a board meeting, or one of its standing committees, the board member is considered to have agreed with any resolution passed, or action taken. The only exception is when such a member has his or her negative vote recorded in the minutes of the meeting.

If the member was not present at a meeting where a decision was made, or an action was taken, with which the member disagreed, the member has the right to deliver, or send by registered mail, a written notice stating the member's disagreement as soon as the member becomes aware of the decision or action. If a member of the governing board does not take the action of recording, or making notification of, a dissent under the requirement of due diligence, the assumption will be that the member agreed with the action taken.

The right to participate and to be informed

Once duly elected, a member of the governing board has the right to attend all meetings of the board. Furthermore, every board member has the right to be informed of all actions and activities which may affect the member in carrying out his or her responsibilities. Even the officers, if authorized to act on behalf of the organization, may not take action on the basis of information obtained without informing all members of the governing board. Failure to inform all the members of the information received, or action taken, can result in a higher level of liability for the participating board members. Board members who were not informed of the information, or action, will not be held liable for such information, or action, provided they were not required to be present at the meeting where such information was received, or such action taken.

For example, members of the audit committee may obtain information from the external auditor about inappropriate entries in the books of account of the organization. Or, the external auditor may suspect that activities, not authorized by the governing board, are taking place and informs the audit committee of such suspicions. Unless the audit committee informs the full governing board of such information received, the members who serve on the audit committee will have breached their duty of diligence. Such members will be liable for any consequences of such failure to inform all the board members.

Relying on other board members

A board member of a charity is not exercising due diligence when leaving everything to others. Relying on the actions and decisions of other board members does not diminish the liability of the board member who relied upon others. Each board member is responsible for all the information and actions of the governing board, unless the board member had no way of knowing about the information or the actions. A board member will not be liable for such misdeeds of other board members if such misdeeds result in damage to the organization, or a third party.

Relying on officers

There is a tendency in charitable organizations for board members to rely on the elected or appointed officers of the organization. It should be noted that board members cannot abdicate their duties and responsibilities to govern the affairs of the organization. This is the common law rule.

In practice, however, board members must usually rely on the chief executive officer of the organization, not only to inform them, but also to implement the policies of the governing board. As such, the governing board must place a great amount of reliance on the chief executive officer.

It is not clear from the common law whether this necessary reliance on the chief executive officer will absolve the board members from liability if he has misled them on the true state of affairs of the organization. The *Caremark International Case* in Delaware which we reviewed above, may be helpful here. As long as the board has "adequate" information and compliance systems in place, they may avoid liability where the board is wilfully misled.

Relying on written reports

Most, but by no means all, legislation dealing with incorporation has provisions allowing directors to rely in good faith on the financial statements of the organization presented to them by an officer of the organization. They may also rely on a written report of the auditor of the corporation, which purports fairly to reflect the financial condition of the charity. This permitted reliance should also extend to a report of a lawyer, accountant, engineer, appraiser, or other person whose profession lends credibility to a statement made by him or her. In jurisdictions where there is no specific legislation for board members to rely on such reports, the common law rules apply.

Because of the exposure to liability, board members should see to it that they receive regular, and detailed, reports about the activities of the organization, as carried out by the chief executive officer and his or her staff. When the board receives such reports, it should make sure that they comply with the board's policies, and all legal and fiduciary requirements. In other words, it is not sufficient for the board to receive reports. Boards have a duty to evaluate such reports in accordance with the standards and duties imposed on board members by specific legislation, or by common law.

Under the common law rules, no method exists by which the governing board may delegate any of the board's powers to officers, or committees of the board.

Relying on outside experts

Although board members cannot delegate any of their responsibilities, they cannot be expected to be experts in all fields of activities in which the organization may be involved. Therefore, governing boards must frequently rely on the opinions, and advice, of specialists, or experts. Governing boards should call upon the expertise of lawyers for legal matters, tax experts for taxation matters, bankers and other financial experts for financial matters, and engineers and architects for building and construction issues. They must exercise their diligence by obtaining appropriate outside advice when circumstances require. However, they exercise diligence in these matters only when they are reasonably assured that the outsider is truly qualified to give the advice, or opinion, sought. For example, it probably would not be considered to be diligent for a governing board to ask a real estate lawyer to give advice to the charity on questions of tax or trust law.

In profit-making corporations, the board of directors may rely on the advice and opinions of outsiders in certain circumstances. These circumstances are,

1. the outsider is independent of the directors,

2. the outsider appears qualified to give advice, and

3. the directors still exercise their own judgement.

It would be safe to conclude, therefore, that even in a for-profit corporation, the person giving advice must be dealing at arms length with the company, and with any other company related to the issue on which advice is sought. Governing boards of charitable organizations must meet at least these three conditions. Too often, boards of charities appoint a lawyer and an accountant to their boards. Then they rely on these experts to advise the board about any legal and tax matters. Such board members are not independent of the board. Reliance on their advice might satisfy the duty of skill of the non-specialist board members, but it would fail the tests of independence and due diligence.

Honorary, alternate, and ex-officio board members

There has been a long-established practice in some charities to appoint certain prominent individuals as honorary members of the governing board. These appointments often are made to recognize a founder or another person who has contributed much time, money, or both, to the organization.

Other organizations have a long-established practice of appointing alternate members to the governing board when the primary member is not able to attend.

In addition, many boards claim that their chief executive officer is a member of the governing board, even if such a member is not entitled to vote because of trust law.

It should be noted that in law there is only one type of board member. All members of a board, no matter what other adjectives are applied to their particular positions, have the same legal duties and responsibilities. Therefore, no one is doing a member, who has served an organization long and diligently, a favour by appointing him or her as a lifetime member of the board, when such a person no longer has the ability to meet the diligence tests. Such an honoured person would be exposed to the same liabilities as every other board member, in addition to the liability of not having exercised due diligence.

The practice of appointing an alternate board member if the primary board member is not able to attend the meeting of the board, poses liability problems for both the primary and alternate board member. Either a person is a member of the governing board and has all the privileges and responsibilities of a board member, or such a person is not a member of the governing board and, therefore, should not be given the right to participate and vote at a board meeting.

I am aware that the practice of appointing alternates has developed in some church denominations which are geographically represented at their major assemblies. The desire was to have equal congregational or regional representation at the meetings of all major ecclesiastical assemblies. Although such a practice may be desirable for ecclesiastical purposes, the translation of this concept to the boards of incorporated and unincorporated charities is inappropriate. Under both corporate and trust law, the alternate board members are as equally liable as the primary board members. As a matter of fact, such primary and alternate board members may have a greater liability, because they are relying on others to make decisions for them.

As to the practice of appointing the chief executive officer as a non-voting, *ex-officio* member of the governing board, it would be better to end this practice. Just because a member of the board is denied the right to vote, does not appear to absolve such an individual from all the duties and liabilities of a board member. It is understandable, and diligent, for a governing board to have the chief executive officer – and possibly other key personnel – attend the meetings of the board, but such staff members should be present only as resource persons. Their function is to report to the board and to receive instructions from the board. Therefore, they are servants of the governing board.

Consequently, it would be inappropriate to saddle them with the duties and liabilities of board members as well.

Doing nothing

Some board members may take refuge in doing nothing, including not speaking or voting at board meetings. It should be noted that doing nothing is no excuse before the law. A board member is not excused for an illegal act just because he or she did not participate in the act.

The courts could conclude that the board member was grossly negligent, willfully blind, or careless in relation to the wrongful act. In such a case, the non-participating board member would be held liable with the participating board members. The courts could also conclude that the board member was not diligent if the illegal act took place at a meeting the board member did not attend, and the board member did not deliver, or send, by registered mail, a written dissent of the act.

Seeing no evil

A board member who obtains knowledge of an illegal act has the responsibility to do whatever is necessary under the circumstances to correct the wrong. Knowledge of such an illegal act may be acquired by reading minutes of meetings prior to the person's appointment to the governing board. It should be clear that a board member takes on all the responsibilities for governance of the organization, including current board policies and activities which were in effect prior to the member's appointment, or election, to the board.

As soon as a board member discovers an activity or policy of the organization, which that board member suspects may be in contravention of any law or government policy, he or she should immediately notify the board in writing of such concern. Such a board member should also request that appropriate action be taken to, either disabuse the board member, or to take corrective action.

Conflict of interest

There are a number of situations which may lead to a conflict of interest for a board member of a charity. In general, conflicts of interest arise only when one of the following occurs:

1. Where board members make a decision which is motivated by
   something other than the best interest of the organization.

2. Where a board member becomes aware of an opportunity to
   make a personal profit when that opportunity could be of benefit
   to the member's organization if it was made fully aware of the
   opportunity.

As far as personal gain is concerned, there is a common law duty
for every board member to act in the best interest of the organization
of which the person is a board member. A board member cannot serve
two masters. If an organization should suffer because of a lack of
regard for all the duties imposed on a board member, the board member could be held liable to the organization. If a board member exercised any power other than in the best interest of the organization,
such an act would be considered a breach of trust. The conflict of
interest subject is dealt with more extensively in Chapter 7.

Liabilities imposed by specific statutes

There are many specific statutes which are of particular interest to
board members of incorporated charities. Board members of charitable organizations should consult their legal and tax advisors to determine what state, provincial or federal legislation affects their organizations. In addition, they should enquire if they have any personal liabilities under such legislation. For example, many jurisdictions make
the board members of charitable organizations personally responsible
for payroll deductions that were not remitted in a timely manner.

Responsibility to creditors

Board members of charities may be liable for debts of a charity,
even after they have resigned as board members. Any creditor may
apply to a court for an order requiring the organization, its board
members, officers, employees, or other agents of the organization to
comply with any provision of any relevant legislation.

In general, for incorporated organizations there is the "corporate
veil" which protects the members of the organization. However, board

members and officers, as agents and trustees of the charity, who are one step removed from the corporate veil, could be deprived of such immunity.

Board members may be held liable to third parties for misrepresenting their authority or acting outside of the scope of their authority. If it is established that they exceeded their authority, board members may also be held liable to the organization.

Indemnification and insurance

Incorporated charities in most jurisdictions have the legal right to protect their board members from the costs incurred for defending themselves from actions because they are members of the board, except in cases arising out of wilful neglect or default.

The indemnity must be specifically given by the organization and is not an automatic right. In general, indemnification of a board member will be legal only if the board member acted in good faith with a view to the best interest of the organization. However, the board member must have reasonable grounds for believing that the action was legal to be able to claim such indemnification.

It should be noted that courts have construed the term "wilful default" to include default which may have been unintentional, and which may have arisen from forgetfulness. Such unintentional default may include an act that is taken without the kind of care that would reasonably be expected from a careful person in looking after his or her own affairs.

Charitable organizations should make sure that their bylaws authorize board members and officers to be indemnified against actions where permitted by the legislation under which the organization exists and operates. Failure to have such provision included in the bylaws could result in board members and officers being denied the right of indemnification.

Usually, insurance is recommended to back up any form of indemnity. The question of whether directors' and officers' liability insurance ("D & O insurance") should be purchased is a matter of risk management. To my knowledge, there are no recorded cases of a successful legal action taken against board members of a charitable organization in their function as board members of the organization, where it was shown that the board members acted in good faith, and in the best interest of the organization. The reality for a charitable organization is that a board member is more likely to be removed for poor judgement than that the board member will be sued.

In the case of a charitable organization, whether incorporated or not, there is an unresolved question whether a charity is authorized to purchase D & O insurance for the protection of its board members and officers. The use of charitable funds to protect board members and officers of an unincorporated organization could be considered to contravene the requirement that all funds are to be used exclusively for charitable purposes.

It may well be that trust law would deem the expenditure for D & O insurance to be an improper expenditure. Board members of charities have a duty to fulfill their responsibilities as trustees. They could be considered to be in breach of trust if they spend trust money buying insurance to protect themselves. The Public Guardian and Trustee of the province of Ontario has taken this position.

On the other hand, arguments could be made that purchasing D & O insurance is no different than reimbursing board members for their out-of-pocket expenses on behalf of the charity. Providing D & O insurance can be said to be a cost incurred in order to attract new board members. Without D & O insurance, many individuals would not accept the risk of being exposed to litigation when they have acted in good faith in compliance with all their duties.

It should be noted that D & O insurance does not cover the biggest damages, such as conflict of interest situations, where a profit has been made by a board member. Most D & O insurance policies are limited to cover only "lawful" acts of the directors and officers of the organization. Since board members of charities are also deemed to be trustees, "wilful default" in carrying out a duty would appear to exclude all such breaches from D & O coverage. For example, it is unlikely that a board member of a charity could be indemnified under D & O coverage when the board member acted in good faith, but did not attend all meetings of the board, where the matter causing the liability was decided, without valid reasons.

Property and casualty insurance

The board also must make sure that sufficient property and casualty insurance is in place to cover the charity's physical assets, and to protect the charity from general liability. If the board does not take proper care that such insurance is in place, the board members could be held personally liable for not being diligent in protecting the charitable resources of the organization. It is reasonable to expect board members to take all available precautionary measures to assure that the charity's assets are protected.

Financial controls and permitted investments

Closely related to the requirement to protect the physical assets of the charity is the requirement to protect the monetary assets. Because the charity holds all its monetary resources in trust for its charitable purposes, the board is required to safeguard such assets as well. Most charities, especially those which submit themselves to external audits, normally have good financial supervision and controls in place for their operating funds. However, such is not always the case for the organization's surplus, or restricted funds.

Most boards have a policy to safeguard any capital which is not immediately needed, or which constitutes the corpus of the restricted funds. Therefore, boards will normally allow such funds to be invested only in secure types of investments. They will choose safe investment such as savings accounts and guaranteed investment certificates. With such investments, the charity has a minimum exposure to loss. If the charity is not exposed to loss, then the board members also have very limited liability exposure.

However, investing so that the capital is safe, may not be sufficient in an age where trustees are required to balance their responsibilities to the capital beneficiaries with their responsibilities to the income beneficiaries of trusts. In some jurisdictions, trustees are required to invest trust funds in a way that a "reasonably prudent person" would invest such funds if they belonged to that person. Since trust law also applies to funds which a charity holds, this requirement would also apply to a charity's surplus, or restricted funds. As a result of this more recent prudent investment test, governing boards of charities will look for investment instruments which balance security with reasonable returns.

In the current financial markets, very sophisticated instruments and fund pools have been developed which are attractive to charities and their boards. The charity's board wishes to ensure that the invested funds produce a reasonable return to assist the charity to carry out its charitable purposes. Therefore, charities frequently invest their surplus and restricted funds in investment pools such as mutual funds, segregated funds, or pooled bond funds. These funds frequently are large and are managed by top quality investment managers. The risks associated with such funds are only marginally greater than investing in government bonds, but the returns, usually, are substantially better.

Although such investment arrangements may appear to be sound, boards should be aware that a charity which has received gifts from the public for its charitable purposes, received such funds in trust. Therefore, the charity is the trustee of such funds. As trustee, the charity, under trust law, may not be able to delegate the administration of such funds to a third party. Since the charity does not make the decision as to which investments will be made by the pooled fund, the charity has relinquished control over its trust funds. Some jurisdictions have legislation specifically allowing trustees to invest in pooled funds. Without the proper legal authority to invest in pooled funds such as mutual funds and segregated funds, the board members may be exposed to liability for misappropriating trust funds.

Therefore, boards should be aware that they can approve investments of the charity's funds only in investments specifically approved for trustees, or over which the board has direct control. It might be interesting to note that indexed funds listed on a stock exchange are considered to be investments over which the investor exercises direct control.

Conclusion of the responsibilities for board members

The common law duties of honesty, loyalty, care, diligence, skill, and prudence required of board members have developed over centuries. These duties have been imposed on directors of corporations, and board members of charities, by the courts to protect the interests of the various interest groups of the corporation, or organization.

For some, the standards required of a board member have become so onerous that they no longer wish to serve on voluntary boards. For others, these requirements have resulted in seeking protection from potential liability by obtaining "directors and officers liability insurance." Such insurance will not protect a board member from breaching one of the common law duties, i.e. the duty of honesty, the duty of loyalty, the duty of care, the duty of diligence, the duty of skill, and the duty of prudence.

In general, board members should not fear the duties imposed on them by common law. As long as they meet the common law requirements (which are not onerous) they should be protected from legal liability. On the whole, the duties required of a board member are based on common sense. It is only in recent legislation for profit-making corporations in some jurisdictions, that higher standards are imposed requiring a director to act like a "reasonably prudent person." The meaning of this phrase has not yet been defined by the courts. But it would appear that a director, at minimum, will not be able to invoke the defence of lack of knowledge, or experience in a specific area.

Although the "reasonably prudent person" legislation has not yet been applied to charitable organizations in most states and provinces at this time, it seems to be prudent for a board member to show that the member made every reasonable effort to become educated in the matter before voting in favour of a particular course of action.

A board member who acts in the best interest of the organization, without personal conflict, has nothing to fear from the duties imposed by the common law. However, it must be remembered that a board member must act in the best interest of the organization. This means that the board member at all times, whether present at meetings or not, is considered to be an active participant in the activities of the organization.

Questions for consideration

To determine the level of exposure a board member of a charity may have to legal liability, each of the following questions or statements should be responded to with a "yes." If one or more of the questions or statements receive a "no" answer, you may be exposing yourself to unnecessary liability. Immediate action should be taken to eliminate the exposure. Such action not only is in your best interest, but it is also in the best interest of the charity.

Some questions or statements will require a percentage estimate, while others require a yes or no answer. Responses to questions or statements requiring a percentage should be as close as possible to 100%.

1. What percentage of board meetings did you attend during the past twelve months?   ___%

2. What percentage of board committee meetings, to which you were assigned, did you attend in the past twelve months?

___%

3. I have not received a salary or any payment for a supply or service from the charity in the past year while I was a board member.

___yes ___no

4. No employee of the charity is an immediate family member such as a brother, sister, father, mother, son, daughter or in-laws.

___yes ___no

5. I have not served more than six year consecutively on the board.

___yes ___no

6. I actively participate in board discussions.   ___yes ___no

7. If I abstain from voting, I have my reasons recorded in the minutes.   ___yes ___no

8. Unless I abstain with reasons, I participate in every vote coming before the board or a committee.   ___yes ___no

9. I have informed myself of the duties of a board member by reading or attending a board orientation session. ____yes ____no

10. I participate in all board meetings with independence of mind and am not required to obtain approval for my actions, or vote, from another party ____yes ____no

11. If the situation would arise where I become privy to information which could affect the organization, I would share such information with the full board ____yes ____no

12. I will, or where applicable did, report all conflict of interest situations in accordance with the board approved policy
    ____yes ____no

13. I come to board meetings fully prepared; I always read the agenda and all supporting documents ____yes ____no

14. I understand, and, at all times, respect the boundaries of the proper relationship between board and staff. ____yes ____no

15. The board does not have alternative, honorary or *ex officio* members? ____yes ____no

16. Does the organization have an annual membership meeting with minutes recorded for such meetings? ____yes ____no

17. The board annually determines that its insurance is sufficient and appropriate to protect its assets, employees and volunteers.
    ____yes ____no

18. The board has an indemnification policy in its governing documents. ____yes ____no

19. The board has officers and directors liability insurance in place.
    ____yes ____no

20. Does the board periodically enquire from the CEO whether all statutory requirements and remittances have been made?

___yes   ___no

21. Does the board approve and monitor the annual operating budget, and does it evaluate the periodic financial results and anticipated expenditures for the remainder of the budget year to determine the organization's fiscal soundness?   ___yes   ___no

Six

Hiring the Chief Executive Officer

and Hiring Policies for Other Staff

In previous chapters, the responsibilities of charity board members were described. It was seen that board members have a wide range of duties, and that they remain ultimately liable for all actions of the charity.

We also saw that, especially in larger organizations, it would be unreasonable to expect volunteers to implement the governing board's objectives and policies. It is realistic for board members to perform all tasks only in the smallest charitable organizations. This chapter, therefore, will discuss the relationship between the governing board, which establishes and supervises the objectives and policies of the charitable organization, and the staff, which implements the decisions of the governing board.

The CEO

To be able to establish a proper relationship between the governing board and the staff, it is important that the governing board select and appoint a chief executive officer ("CEO") to be primarily responsible for implementing board objectives and policies and to be the primary communication link between the governing board and the staff.

In most cases, such a position will have to be a paid position in order to attract a properly qualified person. Since a board member may not receive any remuneration, the position of CEO (unless it is filled by a volunteer) must be held by a person who is not a board member. The CEO in effect becomes the chief agent and usually the chief spokesperson for the charitable organization.

The CEO's job description

Because of the responsibilities which the governing board must delegate to the CEO as its chief agent, it is important that a very clear and concise job description is created for that position. The job description should contain at least the following elements:

1. *Supervision.* It should be clear whether the CEO reports directly to the governing board, the executive committee, or the chairperson.

2. *General Purpose.* A short statement describing that the individual will be the CEO and will be responsible for implementing all board objectives and policies.

3. *Responsibilities.* This section describes all major responsibilities of the CEO position.

4. *Contacts.* Identifies who the CEO has contact with and why.

5. *Minimum Requirements.* This section is divided into two parts consisting of education and experience.

   Education: Specifies the amount of formal education, or its equivalent, which the responsibilities of the position require.

   Experience: 1. *Prior:* Identifies the type and minimum amount of experience that a person, having the necessary education, must have to qualify for the position.

   2. *On-the-job:* Identifies how long it will take to train the individual before he or she will be able to perform effectively and efficiently as CEO.

   3. *Other:* Identifies any other special skills or requirements to perform effectively as CEO. In

religious organizations, this may include a statement as to the requirement that the incumbent have religious knowledge and commitments.

6. *Position Specifications:* This section is included as an attachment to the Position Description and gives supporting position data, information, and illustrations to assist the governing board in evaluating the CEO in his/her continued discharge of duties and responsibilities.

When the position description has been completed, it should be informative to the reader, and must be completely descriptive without being wordy. The position content has to be brought out accurately and precisely. It should not be necessary for the readers to draw upon their imagination, or external knowledge, to understand, or interpret, the CEO's responsibilities. Consequently, examples or illustrations of the CEO's responsibilities are included in the Position Specifications, and are submitted to the governing board to assist in evaluating the position description of the CEO.

Hiring the CEO

Once the Position Description has been approved by the governing board, the process of identifying, interviewing, and hiring the CEO can begin.

So that the governing board can show that it exercised diligence in hiring its CEO, it is important that the search be as broad as possible. The temptation to hire a known friend or former board member should be avoided. This does not mean that such a friend or former board member may not end up as the CEO. In the best interest of the organization, the objective should be to hire the best person possible. If, at the end of that process, a friend or former board member is hired, both the selected person and the governing board will be assured that the best person is filling the position after due competition. Not only does this approach prove that the governing board showed due diligence in their selection of the CEO, but it also enables the CEO to be assured and confident that he or she was the best person for the job.

The search committee

To commence the hiring process, the governing board should appoint a search committee. This committee should receive the mandate

1. to obtain applications from as many prospects for the position as possible,

2. to select for interview those candidates which meet the minimum requirements set by the board,

3. to pre-interview all candidates that meet the minimum requirements,

4. to obtain references on those candidates who meet the minimum requirements once they have passed the pre-interview, and

5. to present to the board a report on all candidates which meet the board's minimum requirements, and which have passed the search committee's preliminary interview.

To give the governing board a true choice, every effort should be made that at least two candidates are presented to the full board with complete application, interview, and reference reports.

To make sure that the search procedure is as objective and fair as possible, it is important that certain procedures are followed. There are certain legal requirements, such as human rights, employment legislation and regulations, and possibly immigration rules where there are applicants who are not national residents. Governing boards should obtain legal advice for their jurisdiction before commencing the search process.

The search process

Aside from the legal considerations, advertising for the position should identify the main duties and responsibilities, education and experience requirements, and the final closing date for applications to be received. The advertisements should also encourage others to nominate persons they deem qualified for the position.

Once enquiries, nominations, or applications have been received, the designated member of the search committee should acknowledge receipt of the enquiry, nomination, or application and send the candidate a copy of the position description, the organization's governing documents, and a summary of the organization's major policies.

In the case of an enquiry or nomination, a member of the search committee should be designated to contact or write the candidate to determine the suitability of the person for the CEO position. If the search committee member determines that the enquirer, or nominee, shows potential to fill the position, the member should encourage the enquirer, or nominee to make a formal application. This should include a short essay describing how the candidate understands the mission of the organization, the requirements of the position, and the procedures to be used to achieve the board's objectives in accordance with its policies. Care should be taken to inform the enquirer, or nominee, that this request for information only places the candidate's name in the pool of prospective candidates, and that there is no assurance that the candidate will be selected.

Those who have applied for the position in response to an advertisement should also be asked to submit a short essay about the candidate's vision for the position in the context of the organization's charitable purposes and strategic plan.

When the closing date for applications has passed, the search committee should review all applications and reject those which do not meet the minimum criteria. Such applicants should be sent a letter to thank them for their interest in the organization and position. They should be informed that other more qualified candidates have applied.

The pre-interview

The remaining candidates should be subjected to further screening consisting of a pre-interview. Whenever possible, this pre-interview should be conducted in person; however, at times the cost of travel may be prohibitive necessitating a telephone interview. Whichever interviewing method is used, care should be taken that relevant information is obtained from the applicants. The interview should consist of at least three parts:

1. The applicant's knowledge of the organization and how the candidate is compatible with the organization's stated objectives, mis-

sion, philosophy, and commitment. This section of the interview concentrates on the personal characteristics of the applicant and should seek to discover personal strengths and weaknesses.

2. The applicant's educational background and work experience. Questions should be asked to clarify or elaborate on the information contained in the application.

3. The applicant's vision for the organization and how the applicant hopes to achieve the board's goals in accordance with its stated policies. This section of the interview seeks to expand on the submitted essay. The focus should be to determine the compatibility of the applicant with the mission and culture of the organization.

Before the pre-interview is concluded, enquiries should be made as to the applicant's salary expectations, and any questions or concerns the applicant may have about the organization, or the position description.

Once all the applicants have been pre-interviewed, the search committee should send a written "thank you" to the applicants for submitting themselves to this procedure. Those who are eliminated at this stage should be informed of this. The remaining applicants should also be informed that they are still being reviewed, and that the search committee will obtain and evaluate references as the next step in the process.

Obtaining references

This is the stage of the selection process that is easily mishandled. Frequently, references are limited to receiving written letters from persons selected by the applicants. It is questionable whether such references are meaningful. Most likely, these references are helpful only for what they do *not* say. Letters of reference provided by the applicant are usually those which the applicant has read and which supply information acceptable to the candidate.

A more useful source of reference is a telephone interview with individuals who have a good knowledge of the applicant, both in relation to the applicant's personal characteristics and job performance. The following check list may be of help in obtaining useful information.

Character references:

1. I wish to obtain some information about (name) whom we are considering for an executive position. How long have you known (name)?
2. In what contexts have you interacted with (name)?
3. How well does (name) get along with other people?
4. Do you consider (name) to be a leader or follower?
5. Does (name) have strong opinions and commitments?
6. Does (name) have any health, or personal, weaknesses, or problems which would concern you by placing (name) in this responsible position?
7. Are there any other comments you would like to make about (name)?

Employment references:

1. I wish to verify some of the information given to us by (name) whom we are considering for the position of CEO of our organization. Do you remember (name)? What were the dates of (name's) employment with your organization? [Do dates check with the application?]
2. What was (name) doing when (name) started with your organization? [Did the applicant exaggerate on the application?]
3. What was (name) doing when (name) left your organization? [Did the applicant progress in previous employment situations?]
4. (Name) says that (name's) salary was $ per _____ when (name) left your organization. Is that correct? [Did the applicant give accurate information on the application?]
5. What was the basis of (name's) compensation? [Any profit sharing? Bonus? Evidence of ownership?]
6. What did you think of (name)? [Did the applicant get along with superiors?]
7. Did (name) have any supervision of others? [Does this check out?]
8. How well does (name) handle supervision? [Is the applicant a leader or a driver?]

9. How closely was it necessary to supervise (name)? [Was the applicant hard to manage or in need of constant help?]

10. How willing was (name) to accept responsibility? [Did the applicant seek responsibility or fear it?]

11. Did (name) have any responsibility for policy formulation? If yes, How well did (name) handle it? [Did the applicant display good judgment? Was the applicant realistic? Was the applicant able to plan ahead?]

12. Did (name) develop or initiate any new plans or programs? [Did the applicant display initiative or creativity? Was the applicant realistic in planning and program development?]

13. How well did (name) "sell" ideas? [Does the applicant show self-reliance? Does the applicant have the ability to adjust to the needs of others?]

14. How well did (name) work? Did (name) finish what (name) started? [Is the applicant habitually industrious and/or persevering?]

15. How well did (name) plan his/her) work? [Is the applicant efficient? Did the applicant display ability to plan?]

16. How well did (name) get along with other people? [Is the applicant a trouble maker?]

17. How much time did (name) lose from work? [Is the applicant conscientious? Does the applicant have health problems?]

18. Why did (name) leave your organization? [Did the applicant have good reasons for leaving previous employment? Do they check with the information given on the application?]

19. Would you re-employ (name)? [Does this affect the applicant's suitability with our organization?]

20. Did (name) have any domestic or financial difficulties which interfered with (name's) work? [Does the applicant display personal immaturity?]

21. What are (name's) outstanding strong points?

22. What are (name's) weak points?

23. For what type of position do you feel (name) is best qualified?

When all references have been obtained, the search committee meets once again to evaluate and tabulate the results. Applicants not deemed suitable for the CEO position after the references have been checked are sent a letter thanking them for their willingness to take part in the selection process and informing them that their names are not among the finalists being submitted to the board. The applicants who have survived the search committee process are informed that they have been declared candidates, and that their names are being submitted to the governing board. These people are informed of the number of names being submitted, if more than one, and that they will have to submit to a formal interview to be arranged by the board at a mutually convenient time and place.

The search committee should send its final report to the governing board together with complete files on each candidate. If possible, the search committee should rank the candidates in order of their deemed qualifications for the CEO position.

Where the search committee was not able to deem any candidate as being well suited for the position of CEO, the committee's report should clearly indicate this fact.

Board interview

When the governing board receives the report from the search committee including the files on each candidate, the board should first determine whether the list provided should be further shortened or whether all candidates should be interviewed. Where there are many candidates, the board may, by voting, decide to interview the top two candidates first.

Whatever the interviewing procedure used, the primary task of the full board interview is to determine the compatibility of the candidate with the board, and the organization. The board should be able to count on the search committee having submitted as candidates only those persons who are qualified, unless the committee has reported otherwise. The amount of work the board has to spend on each candidate's file, and the nature of the interview, will be determined by the strength of the report from the search committee.

As a final step in the hiring process, the board will have to select a final name by vote of all the board members. In some organizations, the selection of a CEO is considered so important that the board requires a two-thirds majority vote for appointment.

The appointment

After the board members have selected the successful candidate, a decision needs to be made on the appointment terms; will the new CEO be appointed with a probationary period, or will an initial appointment of two to five years be extended. There is no single correct answer to this question. The length of the initial appointment time may be influenced by the board members' level of certainty about the selected candidate. If there was uncertainty about the ability of the selected candidate, a two-year appointment period may be appropriate, but the selected CEO needs to be given the time and authority to implement his or her vision, provided that this vision must always be within board objectives and policies. It would be inappropriate to appoint a new CEO on a probationary contract. That would be stating to the candidate and the community that the board has no real confidence in its selection. In that case, it would be better not to make an appointment and to begin the search process all over again.

Having made the decision regarding initial appointment, the starting salary and benefits need to be determined. (It is assumed that a salary range is already in place for the CEO position.) Nothing is wrong with starting a new CEO, without previous CEO experience, at the bottom of the CEO salary range; however, it would be inappropriate to pay an experienced CEO at that rate.

When the terms and conditions for appointment have been concluded, they should be communicated to the successful candidate. The candidate must be given a period of time to decide whether the employment offer will be accepted.

The appointed candidate should also be made aware of the periodic review and evaluation process which the board must adopt. The review and evaluation should be related exclusively to the position description. This is another reason why the position description should be precise. It should be understood, however, that the governing board has the power, from time to time, to change the position description. However, it should be made clear that such changes will be made only in relation to changes in the board's objectives and policies, and not because of the person filling the position of CEO. The new CEO has the right to know what is expected of him, or her, and what the review and evaluation criteria will be.

If the candidate accepts the appointment, a contract should be drawn up with the help of the organization's solicitor. This contract should include all the appointment conditions and details of the compensation package. The board should make sure that the candidate has the opportunity to review the proposed contract with his or her own lawyer. It is possible that some amendments will be suggested by the candidate's lawyer. This contract negotiation period should not be viewed as a threat but as a healthy process giving both parties clarity as to their respective expectations.

When the contract has been signed, the announcement of the appointment can be made.

Conclusion on hiring the CEO

The selection and hiring of the CEO is dealt with in some detail, so that charitable organizations will have a guideline for this process. It has been my experience that the appointment of a CEO, one of the most important decisions to be made by a governing board, is frequently done in a less than professional manner. By following a systematic and objective approach, the organization is more likely to select the right candidate.

Whatever the organization's situation, care should be taken that the governing board gives the CEO the authority to work in accordance with the job description and mandate assigned to him or her. One of the worst experiences for a new CEO is to be faced with board members who continue to meddle in implementing board policies. This activity, while understandable, is inappropriate for board members. Board members will have to continually watch themselves, leaving responsibilities assigned to the CEO delegated, once that action has been taken.

The new CEO must understand that it is very difficult for a board which was previously a policy implementing body, as well as a policy making body, to let go of the daily operations of the organization. To help board members to become comfortable with that new reality, it may be necessary for the new CEO to do more communicating with the board members in the initial stages than would normally be required. However, such communication should not include too much detail, or it may lead to the danger that some board members who previously looked after a specific area will constantly question the CEO's approach and methods.

Board members should remember that during the regular review and evaluation procedure, the new CEO's changes and development should be discussed. But the CEO must be given time and space to develop his, or her, own style and yes, to make his, or her, own mistakes from which the CEO will learn.

Hiring other staff

As stated earlier, the CEO should be the only contact for communication between the board and the staff. This should also mean that the responsibility for the staff rests with the CEO. This does not mean that the board has no right to communicate directly with other staff members, but such communication should always take place with the knowledge and support of the CEO. Failure to observe this fundamental board-staff relationship can result in reporting confusion, which, inevitably, will lead to inefficiencies in implementing board objectives and policies.

Since the responsibility for staff rests with the CEO, it is reasonable to assign the hiring and dismissal responsibilities for administrative or service staff members to the CEO. Only in rare circumstances should the board be involved in hiring administrative or service staff members. Board involvement in hiring, if it exists at all, should be limited to those who hold very senior positions, such as senior department directors, vice-presidents, or persons who are involved in a crucial area of the organization's mission, such as pastors, teachers, and missionaries.

Concern is sometimes expressed by board members of young, growing organizations that they are not able to exercise their duties as board members if they are not directly involved in the hiring of all staff members. Such concerns are usually raised by board members who were previously very active in the implementation of the board's objectives and policies. It is sometimes difficult for such, previously active, board members to retreat to their remaining responsibilities of setting objectives and developing policy. However, for the health and prosperity of any growing organization, which has appointed a CEO, the board members have to withdraw from implementing board policy. Board members have the opportunity to review the activities of the organization on a regular basis – every time the CEO meets with, and reports to, the board.

Only when the CEO has been given the complete authority and accountability for the implementation of board objectives and policies, can the CEO be held accountable for all such activities. To the extent that the board allows linkages between itself and other staff members, the CEO cannot be held accountable for the activities and performance of such staff members.

Although the board delegates the task of hiring all staff below the CEO rank to the CEO, the board should establish the employment policies for the organization. These policies range from establishing qualifications for hiring, to appeal procedures for terminated employees.

Policy development

It is important that a governing board establish clear procedures regarding setting objectives, developing policy, and monitoring the organization's activities. There is a tendency for boards to impose goals and objectives from above. Such attempts may meet with resistance and frequently prove to be counter productive. Without relinquishing its policy development task, the board can encourage the enthusiastic acceptance of board objectives, policies and monitoring. This can be achieved if those primarily affected by the changes or developments are involved in the process. This should mean that staff members will be involved in all policy development which they will have to implement. Therefore, one of the first policies that should be developed is a policy to regulate the procedure by which operational plans are developed, and how the implementation of such plans is to be monitored by the board.

Qualifications

Before staff members are recruited or hired, the governing board should establish the general qualifications and requirements a candidate must meet. This is important to make sure that the candidate accepts the philosophical and/or religious commitment and direction of the organization. Such conditions should include compliance with any staff conduct policy and conflict of interest policy. The qualifications and conditions must be reasonable in relation to the tasks which the employee is required to perform. The qualifications and requirements must also be consistent with the purpose, objects and mission statement of the organization.

For an organization which does not subscribe to a particular statement of faith, employment qualifications and conditions would be fewer than for an organization based on a faith commitment.

Staff conduct policy

To demonstrate that a governing board has developed a reasonable conduct policy for the organization, such a policy must be reviewed in relation to existing legislation. For example, all jurisdictions in the United States of America and Canada have some form of human rights legislation. Such legislation typically denies the right to discriminate on the basis of religion, ethnic origin, colour, sex and age.

Most religious organizations are, at least partially, exempt from the prohibition to discriminate on the basis of religion. In the United States of America this exemption exists because of the separation between church and state. In Canada, human rights legislation exempts religious organizations from the prohibition against discrimination on the basis of religion. However, such an exemption applies only in job positions where the individual's religious beliefs can influence the work to be performed. For example, not a single court in the United States of America would decide that a church discriminated against an applicant for a pastor's position if the individual did not have the same set of religious beliefs as that of the church. However, the response of the court might be quite different if the janitor's job was involved.

The staff conduct policy itself does not deal with discrimination on the basis of certain human and faith conditions. By its very title, it deals with how employees are required to conduct themselves. Such employee conduct requirements may be restricted to the workplace, or they may also apply to an employee's conduct outside the workplace. For example, many organizations prohibit substance abuse. The use of certain substances like drugs usually affects an individual's job performance. Therefore, the staff conduct policy may require that the individual not use prohibited substances.

Another area that needs to be dealt with in the staff conduct policy is the issue of harassment in general, and sexual harassment in particular. If a staff member of a charity were charged with sexual harassment, there is a strong possibility that the organization and its governing board also will be charged. The case against the board could be based on the allegation that the organization did not have a comprehensive policy in this particular area, or that the board did not sufficiently discharge its supervision and monitoring responsibilities.

The staff conduct policy should be very clear. It should form part of any hiring policy and procedure. The courts have held that an employee has the right to know what is expected both in relation to the specific job qualifications required to do the job, and the general qualifications required to fit into the organization. The employee also has the right to know the extent to which he or she will be required to promote its philosophy and/or faith commitment.

A staff conduct policy should include at least the following elements:

1. A statement outlining the organization's ethical and moral standards.

2. Evidence that the person will comply with all applicable laws and regulations which relate to the activities carried out for, and on behalf of, the organization.

3. A commitment that the organization's funds and property at all times must be used for the legitimate objects and purposes of the organization. This commitment must be in accordance with the governing documents, and within the board approved policies.

As noted earlier, it is not sufficient to have a staff conduct policy. The board of the charity must also require management to provide it with regular reports as to how the conduct policy is applied. There has been a court case where a clear staff conduct policy had been passed by the governing board, but where the board and management did not prescribe precise procedures as to how that policy should be communicated to the staff. As a consequence, the court ruled that employees were not subject to the conduct policy because the organization could not show that it had been consistently applied. Without a clear direction as to how to implement and communicate the policy, the board runs the risk that new staff members are not adequately informed of such a policy. From a psychological point of view, many senior staff members will shy away from presenting a staff conduct policy unless a clear procedure is in place. The reason for such "shying away" usually is not that senior staff members disagree with the policy, but because such a policy deals with personal and negative issues which are not very pleasant to bring forward and draw attention to.

The governing board can assure itself that the staff conduct policy will be communicated to all its staff members by requiring each member to sign a copy of the conduct policy. Furthermore, the board can protect itself from allegations that such a policy is not consistently applied and monitored by requiring management to report to the board all incidents where policy breaches occur. In this area particularly, I have experienced a reluctance on the part of senior management to share such information with the full board. Motivated by compassion for the offending staff member, senior management frequently will try to "contain the damage and hurt." This is understandable, but dangerous. Board members may be held liable for certain actions of staff members. If senior management withholds information from the board, they can expose the organization, themselves and the board to greater liability if charges are filed in the courts.

The board, at minimum, should assign the monitoring and compliance procedures of the staff conduct policy to a committee of the board such as a human resource committee, or the executive committee. Such a committee should receive full details of the accusations made against a staff member, and should work with senior management to make sure that the issue is dealt with in accordance with applicable laws. The committee should report the incident, not necessarily with names and all the details, to the full board. It should show the board how it is dealing with the issue. If the board has such a compliance and monitoring system in place, the board members are not likely to be exposed to personal liability.

Staff conduct in the case of close private human interaction

A specific area of staff conduct which frequently causes difficulties for charities, which are involved in counselling, or other one-to-one services, is that of sexual harassment or impropriety. There have been cases in which, in addition to the individual being charged with the impropriety, the organization, and the board, have also been charged. The basis for the accuser extending the charge to the organization and its board, is the allegation that the organization and its board have not sufficiently screened the individuals who are appointed to perform the one-to-one human interaction service for the organization.

When such a charge is made, it is very costly to defend. Worse yet, should the charge of insufficient screening of staff members be upheld in a court, the charity may be faced with significant costs which may not be covered by the organization's liability insurance policy. Unlawful acts are excluded from coverage under most such policies.

To guard against such charges, boards should insist that background checks are performed on all staff members who provide even limited one-to-one services to the organization's clients. By ordering such checks, the board can prove that it acted prudently, and with due care and prudence, in its hiring practices. Such a policy will serve as a defence against charges of insufficient screening.

Types of appointments

When recruiting a prospective staff member, the organization should disclose in a clear manner the type of appointments the successful candidate may receive. For example, an organization may offer all its employees a first appointment subject to a six-month review. Or, an organization may have both term appointments (an appointment for a specific period of time) or regular appointments (an appointment leading to continuing or long-term employment, also called a permanent contract by some organizations).

Recruiting procedures

The personnel or human resource director, or the CEO or his or her designate if the organization does not have a personnel director, in consultation with the department director, should have the primary responsibility for recruiting a new staff member. If the organization has the policy of opening a position to current staff members for promotion opportunities, the position should be posted internally before any external advertising is undertaken. If the organization has a policy which requires competition between current employees and applicants for an open position, the position should be advertised as broadly as possible.

When applications for an advertised opening are received, the person in charge of personnel recruitment should inform the applicant in writing of the policies and procedures for the appointment of staff, and provide a detailed job description.

With the advice of the department director in whose area the opening exists, the most promising candidates are selected and invited for an interview with the interviewing committee. The committee should include the immediate supervisor and personnel director.

After the initial interview, references should be obtained and checked carefully. The procedure to be used for checking such references should be the same as that described earlier in this chapter under the subheading "Obtaining References" which dealt with the recruitment of the CEO.

There are organizations which require the final candidates to have a second interview with the CEO. When such a second interview takes place, it should be understood that the CEO does not cover the same areas covered by the interviewing committee. The interviewing focus of the CEO should be to probe any discrepancies on the application in relation to information received from references. Another area of focus for the CEO should be the potential compatibility of the candidate with the organization's philosophy, or faith commitment, and/or its conduct policy.

Initial appointment of staff

An initial appointment of a new staff member should be for a specified period of time, with a probationary period of about six months. Such appointments are made by the CEO, or his or her designate, after receiving the advice of the interviewing committee.

The successful candidate is notified of his or her appointment by the person to whom the candidate will report. The terms of appointment and ranking of the appointee on the salary scale (discussed below) for that position should be communicated clearly to the appointee. If the appointee indicates a willingness to consider the appointment, two copies of the contract, including all schedules and employment policies referred to in the contract, should be sent to him or her with a request that the appointee return the copies properly executed no later than a specified date. This is normally within one week.

If the appointee declines the position, the next person on the preference list may be appointed provided such a list was prepared and approved by the CEO, or his or her designate.

Salary scales

Most organizations work with a salary ranking system consisting of salary scales for positions at each level of staff. These levels are broken down into a number of increments determined by factors such as education, experience and performance.

Some organizations have a single salary scale for all employees. Position on the scale is determined by factors other than education, experience and performance. The single salary scale approach of remunerating staff has historically been employed by "faith missions" which believe that their workers need to receive enough money to look after their basic needs of food, shelter, etc. and that these needs are the same for all staff members regardless of position on the staff chart.

For the majority of organizations which pay salaries in accordance with responsibility, education, experience and performance, it is important that salary scales are developed which are both objectively and consistently applied regardless of age, race, marital status, or gender. Most jurisdictions not only have human rights legislation, but also have some form of legislation dealing with employment equity or pay equity. Employment equity laws demand that an organization have a policy which clearly implements the concept of "equal pay for work of equal value." Traditionally, this concept meant that an organization could not pay a female employee less than a male employee when substantially the same work was performed by both. There have been attempts in the province of Ontario to expand the concept to include salary comparisons between other similar organizations in the general area.

It should be remembered that the objective behind the legislation requiring equal pay was to eliminate the statistically lower remuneration paid to females in nearly all job classifications. Now the focus is on salary discrimination in job classifications of positions traditionally occupied by females which are deemed to be of equal value with positions traditionally occupied by males. It has been shown statistically that such discrimination has occurred and is still occurring. However, the methods which were used by the Ontario government to address this inequity could lead to financial problems for some charities. The reason for such financial problems is the increased cost to operate which can be illustrated by the following example:

Many years ago, a certain organization made the decision to flatten the pay scale so that the lowest-level employees would receive more than the average pay for similar positions, and the higher-level employees would receive significantly less than the average pay for similar positions with other employers. The middle-level employees in this organization were primarily female. It was determined that there was pay equity in these positions when compared to all other internal positions. However, if the organization were to compare the middle-level positions to similar positions in another organization, which had a more expanded pay scale, it would likely be found that the average pay was less than that of the organizations with which the positions were being compared. As a result, these middle band salaries would have to be increased. However, as a result of such an adjustment, all other salaries would also have to be increased to maintain internal equity. The net result would be that costs would increase substantially. In addition, the lowest level employees then would be paid substantially more than the average pay for similar positions in the comparison organizations. If this organization is then used as a comparison organization to determine pay equity in the other organization, that other organization would have to increase its salaries at the lower level. This most likely would result in an upward adjustment of all salaries in that organization having the result that the middle and upper salary levels of the first organization may need to be adjusted once again. The net result of this approach would be an ever increasing pay spiral.

The purpose of the above illustration is not to make comments about the political agendas of various governments. Rather, the purpose is to make board members aware of the external pressures that can be brought to bear on an organization which attempts to conduct its affairs in a way that is different from the norm. Organizations and their governing boards should be well informed about the possible consequences of adopting remuneration systems that are out of the ordinary in relation to the social-political climate of the day. Even if all employees voluntarily agree with the approach, pay equity legislation may force the organization to adopt traditional, hierarchical remuneration schedules.

As a result of the foregoing discussion, it is advisable that organizations adopt salary scales which are comparable to other organizations providing similar services. This means that salaries at all levels should be comparable to salaries at all levels in the comparative organizations.

Salary ranks

Aside from the salary scales for the various staff levels of the organization, a clearly defined policy needs to be developed which places all employees at the appropriate salary increment on a specific grid. An organization which does not have such a clearly defined policy of placing employees in a proper rank, leaves itself open to challenges of discrimination.

An organization should determine the criteria to be used for a staff member to move from increment to increment on the salary scale applicable to his or her position. The salary scale may have relatively few (e.g., five to ten) increments, or many more (e.g., ten to twenty). Factors which may be included in determining movement up the increment grid can be the following:

1. *Education*: If level of education achieved beyond the minimum requirement for the position is to be recognized, a determination should be made as to the number of increments that will be allowed for the various levels of education or training. For example, an organization may allow one increment for every full year, or equivalent, of study at university beyond a BA, and one-half increment for each year of study, or equivalent, beyond a diploma program at a junior or community college.

2. *Experience:* Some organizations, especially at lower staff levels, consider experience in other similar positions eligible for placement at a higher rank on the salary scale. If such is the case, the types of experience and increment credit for each year of previous service should be defined clearly. For example, an organization may allow a full increment for each year of identical activity performed with another organization, and one-half increment for each year of related work activity.

3. *Performance*: Some organizations reward employees for their productivity while others consider this approach to be too controversial, leading to internal friction. If performance increments are not allowed, there is no need to be concerned with this issue. If performance increments are allowed, a policy acceptable to all employees needs to be developed. For example, job performance criteria need to be developed for each position in consultation with persons filling those positions. Such criteria may include activities which foster professional growth such as attending certain conferences or seminars, reading relevant literature, and communications with others in similar job situations. It may also involve recognition for service to the community beyond the immediate job requirement.

Once an increment policy has been established by an organization, salary increments should be granted in strict compliance with the policy. In addition, if salary increments are to be withheld for financial reasons, the staff should be consulted, and must agree to such a freeze.

Annual evaluation

The annual employee evaluation is an important activity for the governing board to be assured that proper checks and balances are in place to assure them that all the charity's resources are used efficiently and effectively in the furtherance of its goals and objectives.

All staff evaluations (except the evaluation of the CEO, which is performed by the governing board itself) are performed by, or on behalf of, the CEO.

The supervisor of each staff member prepares an evaluation which covers job performance, interpersonal skills, communication effectiveness, and personal behaviour. In addition, the supervisor should discuss strengths and weaknesses and goals for improvements in areas requiring improvement. The purpose of the annual evaluation is intended to assist professional development, and is not to be seen as disciplinary in nature.

Once the supervisor has completed the evaluation, the staff member should be asked to acknowledge that the evaluation was discussed with him or her by signing the evaluation form, and the staff member should have opportunity to write comments on the evaluation form in areas of disagreement. The staff member should receive a copy of the evaluation form when it has been signed by both the staff member and the supervisor.

Prior to the completion of the supervisor's evaluation of the staff member, the staff member should also evaluate his or her supervisor. Such staff evaluation of the supervisor should be confidential, i.e., the supervisor does not receive a copy of this evaluation; it should be submitted to the supervisor's supervisor. In the case of the CEO, the supervisor would be a member of the governing board, or a committee of the board appointed for that purpose at a meeting of the board.

Although evaluations should be conducted in a professional and thorough manner for all employees, evaluations for supervisory and senior positions should be more rigorous. Employees who interact directly with the organization's clients and the general public should be evaluated more extensively than those who do not have such involvement.

Evaluation for permanent employment

Staff members who are in their initial probationary appointment should be formally evaluated before the end of their probationary period. Any concerns that come to light during the probationary period should be noted in writing in the employee's file, and reviewed at the time of the evaluation for permanent employment.

If there are significant deficiencies, but not sufficient to dismiss the staff member, an extension of the initial appointment, to allow for further development and evaluation, may be granted. Care should be taken that an extension does not exceed a specified period of time (e.g. not more than a total of twelve months). As the maximum probationary period allowed by the organization approaches, a clear decision should be made, either to extend a permanent appointment or to terminate the employee.

Promotion policy

An organization should have a clear policy in relation to job promotion. Such a policy could be that advancement to a higher position is possible only when a vacancy in such a position exists. All staff members will be considered for promotion when an opening occurs, but a vacancy will not necessarily be filled from among those at a lower rank. When opportunities for promotion occur, it should be made clear that staff members may apply for such promotion on their own initiative, or be encouraged for such a promotion by their supervisor. Application for promotion may be made by any staff member when a vacancy occurs if the applicant believes that he or she has sufficient qualifications to perform the required tasks.

Criteria for promotion

To be considered for promotion, a staff member should continue to meet all the basic employment criteria of the organization in addition to showing evidence of being able to work independently. Participation in the organization's activities or programs and demonstrated administrative ability should also be considered.

There are organizations which have different employment criteria for different job categories. For example, a religious organization may require a teacher or counsellor to subscribe to the organizations statement of faith, but not demand that same level of commitment of an individual hired in the clerical or janitorial department. If different criteria are required for different job classifications, those criteria should be in writing and available to all employees in order to avoid a charge of discrimination when an applicant for promotion is denied that promotion, e.g. for lack of compliance with the statement of faith.

Permanent contract or continuing appointment

There are organizations which provide their employees with a permanent contract, or continuing appointment after the initial probationary period has been completed. In most of these situations, the understanding is not in writing, but is assumed on the basis of traditional practice.

There are other organizations which have either a written or verbal policy that any employee can be terminated subject to a period of notice. This notice period usually is the same as that required by the employment legislation in the jurisdiction where the organization's head office is located.

Other situations arise where individuals at different employment levels are treated differently in relation to their continued job security. For instance, a secretary or janitor may be released on two weeks notice, while a teacher may be given a one-year notice.

It is wise to have the policy relating to term of employment in writing unless each employee has a fixed contract which comes up for renewal at a specific time. Failure to have a clearly defined term for each employee or position can lead to uncertainty regarding severance pay entitlement if an employee is terminated for any reason.

Termination of employment

One of the most difficult issues to deal with for any organization is the possibility that an employee may have to be terminated. Termination may be due to a number of factors such as the organization's lack of finances, termination of a program or service, incompetence of an employee, or breach of the organization's policies by an employee. As a result of the wide range of reasons which can lead to termination, some organizations make a distinction between termination where the person is deemed to be "in good standing," and termination where the person is "not in good standing."

Termination in good standing

Termination in good standing is normally restricted to such issues as lack of finances, or termination of a program or service. If an organization is well managed, provisions will normally be in place to assure the staff of continued financial resources for existing programs or services. However, in spite of the best planning on the part of the board and management, situations may arise which are beyond the organization's control, which result in a significant decrease in revenue. Such situations may arise as a result of a drastic reduction in major funding sources such as government grants.

Termination of employment as a result of a change in program or service is more likely with poor planning. It is unlikely that a well planned program or service will need to be discontinued on short notice. This is especially true if a program or service has been in effect for a number of years. Even if a program or service is to be discontinued, another program or service may be started to which some, or all, of the employees of the discontinued program or service may be transferred. However, in the situation of discontinuance of a program or service, a long-time valued employee may have to be released for valid reasons.

In the case of termination of employment resulting from the above two situations, the employee to be dismissed should be continued on salary for as long as possible. Such an employee should also be given every opportunity and assistance to obtain other employment. If the organization agrees to provide the dismissed employee with extended salary (e.g. for a year), it should be made clear that such continued salary will end when the employee finds other gainful employment. Therefore, it will be in the best interest of the organization to do whatever is within its power to assist the dismissed employee in finding new employment. Such employment-seeking assistance would be considered good stewardship of the organization's resources.

Termination not in good standing

More difficult is the situation where an employee needs to be terminated for cause. In such a situation the dismissed employee is not in good standing. Care should be taken when termination for cause relates directly to performance, or conduct incompatible with the statement of faith and conduct policies of the organization. In the case of all such terminations, it is important that procedures used to dismiss an employee are part of the organization's employment policies and that they are available to all employees. Failure to apply such policies consistently, may result in challenges either through human rights commissions, or through the courts. One of the most important considerations, during a legal review of an organization's determination to dismiss or terminate an employee for cause, will be whether "natural justice" was used by the organization. The material in the remainder of this chapter is designed to assist not-for-profit organizations in establishing procedures which are not likely to offend the "principles of natural justice."

If the staff member's professional effectiveness appears to be diminished seriously, the individual's supervisor should discuss that issue with the staff member to try to resolve the difficulty. Failing a resolution, the supervisor should refer the matter to his or her supervisor. The supervisor will initiate a special evaluation procedure consisting of interviewing the staff member and reviewing the documentary evidence supporting the position that the staff member's professional effectiveness has diminished.

After this evaluation, the CEO (or the board appointed committee in case the CEO is under review) should make a decision regarding termination of the staff member. If it is decided to terminate, the terminated staff member should receive a copy of the reasons for termination, and should have the right to appeal, as described under *Appeal procedure*.

In a situation where a staff member's conduct is at variance with the organization's staff conduct policy, the CEO should meet with the staff member to discuss the matter. He or she should also convene a meeting of the senior administrators (in larger organizations), or the committee of the governing board appointed for such purposes (in smaller organizations). If the staff member involved reports directly to the CEO, a committee of the governing board should act in such instances. The senior administrators, or the committee of the governing board, as the case may be, will interview the staff member, who is given an opportunity to respond to the charges, and make a recommendation to the CEO. Upon recommendation of such a committee, the CEO will decide whether the staff member's conduct warrants dismissal, or other appropriate action. The CEO will inform the interviewing committee of the decision reached.

It should be clear that, since the CEO is responsible for hiring all staff, he or she is also the person responsible to dismiss staff members for any reason including dismissals for inappropriate conduct. However, when such dismissal involves persons who report directly to the CEO, the governing board should pass a resolution, confirming the CEO's decision, prior to communicating it to the staff member who is to be dismissed.

Disagreement with the statement of faith

There are organizations such as churches, and similar religious organizations, which have a statement of faith, to which key staff members are required to subscribe. If a staff member who is otherwise in good standing appears to be in disagreement with such an organization's statement of faith, the supervisor should discuss the issue with the staff member to try to resolve the difference. If this discussion does not lead to a resolution, the supervisor will refer the issue to the CEO, who will meet with the staff member to attempt a resolution of the matter.

If it is not possible to resolve the matter either through discussion with the supervisor or the CEO, the CEO should appoint a special committee to review the issue and to advise the CEO. This committee interviews the staff member after obtaining a written submission regarding the disagreement from the staff member. If the committee determines that a resolution of the matter is not possible, it prepares a written report of its advice to the CEO. Since it is the governing board which is charged with maintaining the mission and direction of the organization, the CEO then makes his report together with the committee's advice, to a committee of the governing board called into being for that purpose (e.g. the executive committee), or to the full board.

The committee or the full board, as the case may be, also must interview the staff member to determine whether the difference is sufficient to compromise the organization's mission and direction. If the committee or governing board determines that the difference is sufficient to dismiss the person, it will then advise the CEO to do so.

After obtaining the advice from the special committee and the governing board, or its committee, the CEO prepares a written report to be provided to the staff member, outlining the grounds for termination. The staff member may appeal the decision of the CEO as set out below.

Suspension

A staff member awaiting the outcome of an investigation regarding a disagreement with the statement of faith may be suspended by the CEO, or assigned to other duties, should continuation of normal duties be considered harmful to the staff member, to others, or to the organization. Salary should continue during the period of suspension. Care should be taken that the suspension and related investigation last no longer than three months.

Salary of a dismissed staff member

A staff member who is deemed to be a permanent employee, i.e. one who has completed the probationary appointment period, and who is dismissed while not in good standing, or who is dismissed with cause, may have his or her salary extended or discontinued at the discretion of the CEO, subject to statutory requirements.

Appeal procedure

A staff member who disagrees with the employment decisions of the CEO regarding reappointment, promotion, or termination may appeal such decision to a special committee. This committee would consist of members of the governing board and would be appointed by the board. Written appeals should be sent to the CEO who should immediately refer the appeal to that committee.

The board's appeal committee will meet to hear the appeal. Both the CEO and the staff member may be present at all stages of the hearing. The staff member may be accompanied by a colleague, or other representative, to assist in presenting the case. Both should also have access to all supporting documentation and available evidence.

After hearing all the evidence, the appeal committee deliberates and votes on the decision. If the majority of the appeal committee vote in favour of the staff member, the decision is forwarded to the governing board. If the vote of the committee results in a defeat of the staff member's appeal, there is no further appeal to the governing board.

In the case where the appeal by the staff member has been sustained by the appeal committee, both the original decision of the CEO and the alternative recommendation of the committee are presented to the governing board. After an interview with the staff member, the governing board decides upon the matter by a majority vote of those present. The decision of the governing board is final.

Confidentiality

The evaluation and/or appeal procedure as outlined above is one that requires much integrity and compassion of those involved in it. For people to speak their minds openly, without fear of reprisals, it is crucial that all persons involved in the activities outlined above receive and deal with all verbal and written submissions, and related documents, with the highest level of confidentiality. Confidentiality in these matters is so important that its breach should be considered grounds for suspension or dismissal, depending on its severity as decided by the governing board.

Organizational charts

Every organization with a CEO and other staff members should have a chart which supplies both the board and the staff with a clear picture on their relationship to the total activities of the organization. This chart we will call the "administrative chart." In addition to the staff chart, there should be a chart outlining all committee reporting relationships in the organization. This chart we will call the "committee chart." Together, these two charts show all organizational structures. Each of these charts are discussed below.

Administrative chart

The complexity of the administrative chart depends on the size of the organization. An organization with few staff members requires a very simple administrative chart, while the administrative chart for a large organization may be very complex. However, no matter how large or small an organization may be, there are certain tasks or functions which need to be identified.

It is a common practice to equate the administrative chart with the employees of the organization. In such situations, the administrative chart usually identifies individuals in relationship to superiors and subordinates. Another method of designing the administrative chart is to identify the tasks and functions that have to be performed. These tasks and functions should then be entered on a chart. In such a case, the chart may be more detailed, since one person may perform different tasks which appear separately on the administrative chart. This latter chart we refer to as a function-based administrative chart. Since we believe a function-based administrative chart to be more suited to both growing and larger organizations, our comments will be restricted to developing that type of administrative chart.

A primary issue which needs to be addressed is whether the organization wishes to have a hierarchical structure with many reporting levels, or relatively flat structure with very few reporting levels. Historically, many larger organizations had many levels of reporting relationships. It was believed that many levels of reporting enabled the organization to have more checks and balances. It was thought that this checks and balances structure would prevent costly errors. Although that may be the case, experience showed that such multi-level reporting organizations discouraged innovation and creativity. Besides, they were very expensive to operate. Administrative costs were very high in relation to the primary activities of the organization. Over the past number of years, there has been a complete "rethink" of organizational management. The result is that the flat organizational structure with as few reporting relationships as possible has now become popular. We believe that the fewer levels of reporting there are in an organization, the more effective the organization can be in implementing board objectives and policies. It is our experience that, with rare exceptions, staff initiatives and creativity improve with the level of responsibility given to them. The checks and balances, which any responsible organization must have, can be maintained by means of an effective reporting and monitoring process. Consequently, the administrative chart discussed below has four levels.

To develop a function-based administrative chart for an organization, the following list of common functions and common reporting relationships which need to be plotted on the chart are provided.

1. *CEO*: This function is shown at the top of the chart. If the CEO has an assistant, the assistant's function is placed below and to the side of the CEO's function.

2. *Vice-Presidents or Departmental Directors:* These functions are shown at the second level of the chart; reporting to the CEO. There is usually more than one primary function in any organization (e.g. programs, student services, budget & finance, building & administration, and ancillary services). The number and type of primary departments will depend on the nature of each organization. Whatever the activities of an organization may be, the primary functions should be clearly identified and labelled, even if one individual has responsibility for more than one primary function. For example, if the director of budget & finance also is the director of building & administration, it may be advisable to list both functions separately in order to accommodate future growth and development when the two functions may be split and looked after by two persons. All functions located on the second level should report directly to the CEO.

3. *Assistant Directors or Area Supervisors:* The third level on the administrative chart should be occupied by sub-functions which

require the individuals to report to a second level person because of the nature of their task. For example, under budgeting and finance, there may be an assistant director of budgeting, and an assistant director of accounting. It is important that both functions report to the head of budget & finance, so that this person is able to continually monitor current results in relation to future projections. Similarly, the chairpersons of each of the traditional four faculty divisions in a liberal arts university would report to the academic dean, so that he or she can determine that a proper academic program balance is maintained.

4. *Implementing Functions:* The fourth and final function level of the organization should be the functions which implement the organization's objectives. These functions report to the assistant directors or area supervisors. Persons filling these functions have no others reporting to them within the context of the organization. These functions are the front-line functions where the actual organizational activities take place. For example, in the accounting area, these would be the functions of invoicing, accounts receivable, accounts payable, payroll, etc.; in a school these would be the teaching activities; in a social service organization these would include such functions as counselling and other direct client services.

Committee chart

In Chapter 3, we discussed the need for certain board standing committees. In this section, we will discuss those committees that are set up by, and report to, the CEO or his or her designated staff. To be sure that the committee chart shows all committees involved in the organization, the board and its committees should be shown on the chart as well as the staff committees.

There is no ideal or minimum number of committees that an organization should have. Neither is there a precise method to determine whether a given committee should be *ad hoc* (i.e. to deal with a specific issue that has come up and then disbanded) or continuing (i.e., to deal with continual issues in a given area, such as program development). However, it is important that each committee to be established receive a clearly defined mandate, i.e. a clear statement describing to whom, or to what body, the committee should report. The make-up of the committee should also be clearly defined.

It is not possible to give examples of all committees which an organization could have. There is such a great variety of charitable organizations with different committee needs. For that reason, only two common non-board committees are described:

1. *Finance Committee:* Historically, the finance committee has been viewed as a board committee. The traditional finance committee would have two primary functions consisting of budget and expenditure monitoring, along with external audit relations. In addition, the finance committee quite often would have members which were not board members of the organization. With the advent of a board audit committee, which must be made up of board members only, organizations may wish to have the finance committee report directly to the chief financial officer and/or to the CEO. Such a development is logical, since the CEO is accountable to the board for implementing its objectives and policies. The finance committee should have the following mandate:

   a) To monitor ongoing expenditures in relation to the approved budget.

   b) To assist the chief financial officer in developing an annual budget.

   c) To determine costs of new program proposals and how these will affect the immediate and long term budget.

   d) In consultation with the chief program officer, to advise the chief financial officer on fees, if any, to be charged for products and/or services rendered.

   e) To advise the chief financial officer, or the CEO, on financial policy development.

   f) To monitor financial policy implementation, as approved by the board from time to time.

   g) To monitor all financial reporting and remittances, as required, to be sent to the appropriate government agencies on a timely basis.

2. *Program Committee:* The program committee should report to the chief program officer, and/or the CEO, and should have the following mandate:

   a) To monitor the efficiency and effectiveness of the delivery of products, and/or services to the clients of the organization.

   b) To assist the chief program officer in preparing a plan of action for the ensuing year.

   c) To consult with the chief financial officer on the budgetary effect of proposed program development.

   d) In consultation with the chief financial officer, to determine fees, if any, to be charged to the clients who are the beneficiaries of the organization's programs and/or services.

   e) To advise the chief program officer and/or the CEO regarding program policy development.

The above committees advise management, but they will also initiate policies which ultimately must be approved by the board. The process of sending policy recommendations to the board is by means of the CEO; however, most CEO's will wish to make certain that there is general internal acceptance of policy proposals before they are sent to the board. For this purpose, among others, most CEO's will have an informal, if not formal, cabinet consisting of the CEO and all staff having second-level administrative responsibilities.

Advisors to the CEO

As the primary communication link between the governing board and the staff, the CEO will wish to maintain communication links which assure him or her that the CEO position does not hinder the necessary flow of information. It is difficult for any person to be completely informed at all times on all the details of an organization. This is especially the case in large organizations. To be sure that all necessary information is communicated to the appropriate parties, the CEO normally establishes a cabinet, or an administrative council, which the CEO chairs. For our purposes, we will refer to this body as the cabinet.

The cabinet is established by the CEO to create a formal avenue for communication of board objectives and policies to the various department heads that report directly to the CEO. In addition, it also serves the purpose of collecting minutes and policy recommendations from the various operational committees, and staff departments. The membership of the cabinet is normally restricted to senior personnel who report directly to the CEO. The mandate of the cabinet normally includes the following:

1. To advise the CEO on issues placed before it.

2. To advise the CEO on internal policy implementation.

3. To advise the CEO on implementation of board policy.

4. To advise the CEO on internal policy development.

5. To advise the CEO on board policy development.

6. To review internal committee minutes and reports.

7. To review operational reports intended for distribution to the board and to advise the CEO on their accuracy and completeness.

8. To identify and resolve potential conflicts between operational departments.

Staff attendance at board meetings

In some organizations, the board regularly meets without the CEO present. It is difficult to see how the board can discharge its duty of diligence if the individual members of the board do not have the opportunity to question the CEO directly. Fortunately, the practice of not having the CEO attend board meetings is rare and should be resisted by all boards. The argument sometimes used by boards is that it is difficult to discuss the performance of the CEO when he or she is present at the meeting. The answer to such concern would be to hold a portion of the meeting *in camera* when the performance, or the remuneration of the CEO is discussed.

Although the CEO normally is the only staff member with a right, written into the bylaws, to attend the meetings of the governing board, more progressive boards and CEO's encourage senior staff members who report directly to the CEO, to attend board meetings as additional resource persons. An additional benefit to both the CEO and the organization is that senior staff members gain a better understanding about board policies and objectives. It is very difficult to communicate the desires, concerns, and nuances of the board when the written minutes usually record only board decisions. By being present at board meetings, senior staff members are better able to understand the reasons for certain board actions.

Staff speaking at board meetings

As stated earlier, the CEO normally has a right to attend all board meetings. Since the CEO also should be the primary communication link between the board and the staff, he or she should also have the right to speak at all board meetings. Without the ability to amplify on the written report of the CEO to the board, the CEO would not be able to inform the board members on some of the background information which may not be appropriate to put in writing. In addition, the CEO should be able to question board members on board policy and objectives, so that he or she is better able to understand and communicate to the staff and others on such matters.

The authority for other senior-level staff members to speak at board meetings is a different matter. Whether such staff members should be given the right to speak depends on the comfort level of the board members and the CEO. Certainly, the CEO should have the right to direct some questions, or reporting issues, to the staff members with primary responsibility in the area under discussion. For example, I have attended board meetings where financial reports were presented by the treasurer of the board; however, neither the treasurer, nor the CEO were intimately acquainted with the background information. In such a case, it would be helpful for the CEO to ask the director in charge of finances to speak to the issue.

The key distinction to remember is that the CEO should have a legal right to speak at board meetings, while other staff members have a delegated right to speak – delegated by the CEO.

Absence of the CEO

One always hopes that the CEO will remain healthy and available for all meetings which he or she normally attends. However, sometimes the CEO becomes ill, or for other reasons, beyond the CEO's control, must be absent for an extended period of time. In case this should happen, it is important that the CEO, with the support of the board, establish a policy which defines the authority structure during the absence of the CEO. A possible extended CEO absence policy could be as follows:

1. To have the least disruptive process in the absence of the CEO, the [director of, or Vice-President of] (hereinafter referred to as the "CEO designate") is appointed to act as chairperson of the cabinet and as primary contact person. All decisions will be made by him/her in consultation with the cabinet.

2. Recommendations on non-routine matters should be discussed by the CEO designate with the senior staff member primarily responsible for the issue and with the chairperson of the board. The chairperson of the board (who may consult the executive committee) shall then advise the CEO designate and the senior staff member responsible on the disposition of the matter.

3. The CEO designate is hereby authorized to bind the organization in any contracts which the CEO would have the power to bind the organization if he/she were present, provided that the transactions were approved in accordance with 1. or 2. above.

Questions for consideration

The following questions or statements are designed to determine whether the board exercises proper supervision over the staff. In addition, some of the questions or statements are designed to determine the proper relationships between board and staff. The board remains responsible for the activities of the organization. It may delegate the implementation of board policy to the staff, but it must have policies and procedures in place to make sure that the activities of the organization remain consistent with the organization's governing documents, and with the board's policies.

The action or activity underlying every question or statement that is responded to with a "no" should be reviewed. In this way board members can make sure that it is brought in compliance. When the board takes such actions, it minimizes its exposure to future difficulties or challenges.

1. Is the relationship between board and CEO clearly documented and followed by all board members? ___Yes ___No

2. At every board meeting, the CEO is required to submit a written report of the organization's activities since the previous meeting. ___Yes ___No

3. At every board meeting, the CEO is required to submit for approval any changes in programs or activities when such proposed changes do not fully comply with the board's approved policies and previous approvals. ___Yes ___No

4. The Board, annually, sets clearly defined objectives for the CEO, and requires the CEO to set objectives for all staff so that staff performance evaluations can be measured against such objectives. ___Yes ___No

5. Does the board perform an annual written evaluation of the CEO? ___Yes ___No

6. Does the board have an approved, written hiring and related employment and evaluation policy for all staff and volunteers? ___Yes ___No

7. Does the board have an approved, written conduct policy which must be signed by all staff and volunteers? ___Yes ___No

8. Does board policy require background checks on all staff to be appointed for such tasks as counselling and other one-to-one client or donor services? ___Yes ___No

9. Does the board require its conflict of interest policy to be signed by all staff and volunteers? ___Yes ___No

SEVEN

Developing a Conflict of Interest Policy

A charge of conflict of interest is the greatest liability exposure for a charity and its board members. Conflict of interest is not restricted to a situation in which the board member is personally involved. The board is also responsible for assuring that staff members are not involved in conflict of interest situations. To be able to develop a sound conflict of interest policy, there needs to be clear understanding of what conflict of interest actually is.

Conflict of interest is a much debated issue. There are many opinions of what constitutes conflict of interest. At one end of the spectrum of opinions is a position that conflict of interest occurs only in situations where a board member, or an employee financially benefits from an undisclosed relationship. The opposite end of the spectrum might be that conflict of interest occurs in any situation where a board member, or an employee has any type of interest, either directly, or indirectly, through real dealings or undisclosed relationships. The former position might lead to condoning situations which ought to be avoided, while the latter position may lead to banning very innocent activities. Examples of this kind of result will be dealt with later.

The purpose of this chapter is to discuss some of the issues surrounding conflict of interest. My goal is to discuss some of the issues that need to be considered in developing an effective conflict of interest policy. In the process, I will also attempt to show that charities cannot be in economic conflict – charity to charity – if they wish to remain true to their primary constituency which is the public. The public cannot be in conflict with itself.

Conflict of interest types

It is important to explore both real, and perceived conflict of interest as a background to developing a policy which is both philosophically sound, and workable in practice. In developing a workable conflict of interest policy, it is helpful to make distinctions between the various types of conflict of interest. These conflict of interest positions can be divided into two main types: those that result in material benefit to the board member or employee, and those that result in non-material benefit to such persons. The two main types of conflict of interest can be distinguished as direct, indirect, and perceived benefits. The six levels of conflicts can be presented as follows:

	Material	Non-Material
Direct	1	2
Indirect	3	4
Perceived	5	6

Material direct conflict of interest

It is usually not too difficult to identify a direct material conflict of interest. The employee or member of the governing board would receive a direct benefit, of a material nature, as a result of dealings with the organization, or dealings with a business or organization that supplies goods or services to the organization. Two examples of this type of conflict are:

1. A member of the governing board or an employee receives a kickback, or secret commission, from the company or individual providing a product or service to the organization, or

2. A member of the governing board or an employee receives payments for supplying goods or services to the organization.

It is quite clear that most members of an organization, as well as the general public, will consider these two examples as unacceptable conflicts of interest.

However, such material direct conflict of interest may be a little more acceptable to people when a supplier of a product or service makes a gift available to an individual working for a charity. On the face of it, there is no connection between the gift, and the service or product provided to the charity. The issue that needs to be addressed is the reason for which a supplier would make gifts to employees of customers or clients. What is the supplier's motivation? Normally, such gifts are made by the supplier to endear the employee to that particular supplier so that future purchase decisions are influenced by personal benefits, rather than sound business practices alone. Therefore, gifts from suppliers, other than gifts of nominal value, such as a calendar, or an inexpensive pen, should be avoided.

Non-material direct conflict of interest

This non-material, direct conflict of interest is more difficult to deal with for most organizations. A member of the governing board or an employee receives a direct, non-material benefit in the following two examples:

1. An organization obtains goods or services from a person, or a company owned by a friend of an employee, where it is understood that the friendship with that particular employee was the deciding factor in the selection process.

2. A member of the governing board, or an employee, arranges for, and receives public recognition for, a gift in kind from a friend, where it is believed that the gift is of great benefit to the organization.

Many organizations and individuals would not consider that the organization is placed in a disadvantaged position in either of these two examples. Consequently, these situations would not be seen as real conflict of interest. However, if, in the first example, the goods or services are of substandard quality, the friendship may get in the way of dealing in a business-like fashion. Likewise, in the second example, if the donation consisted of land which was subsequently found to be polluted, and this resulted in substantial clean-up costs to the organization, then the friendship could result in conflict of interest accusations?

Material indirect conflict of interest

Material indirect conflict of interest frequently occurs where a member of a governing board or an employee does not benefit in a direct way. Examples include the following:

1. A family member receives a kick-back or a secret commission from the company or individual providing a product or service to the organization, or

2. An individual or corporation not dealing at arms length with an employee of the organization supplies goods or services to the organization.

Non-material indirect conflict of interest

The concept of non-material conflict of interest results in much debate. Non-material benefit is difficult to define. However, there are situations in which individuals are advantaged by being involved in non-material, indirect conflict of interest situations. Examples include the following:

1. Someone in a position to make purchasing decisions agrees with a supplier to purchase that supplier's goods or services in exchange for a commitment by the supplier to hire a friend.

2. An executive director hires an individual who is related to an executive in another organization, and as a reward for such hiring, the hiring organization receives favourable publicity through the other organization.

Perceived material conflict of interest

Perceptions are difficult to deal with at the best of times. When such perceptions become entangled with conflict of interest, they may take on a life of their own. Perceptions can become destructive for both organizations and individuals. The comment that "perception is reality" takes on special meaning when real situations arise which can be seen to result in negative connotations for persons or organizations. Examples of perceived material conflicts of interests are:

1. Organization A enters into a joint-venture arrangement with organization B and, totally independent of the decisions leading up to the joint-venture arrangement, the spouse of the CEO of organization A is hired as a senior administrator by the CEO of organization B.

2. A business owned by a cousin of an organization's CEO is awarded a contract to supply the organization with a product or service.

Perceived non-material conflict of interest

If perceived material conflict of interest is difficult to deal with, the non-material perceived conflict of interest is even more so. If a material benefit can be identified, there usually is an objective mechanism that can be developed to deal with the situation. In the case of perceptions of conflict of interest that do not result in a material consideration, it is nearly impossible to answer a concern to the satisfaction of the person bringing the charge. Examples of this type of conflict are:

1. A close friend of the CEO does business with the CEO's organization.

2. A person is employed by one organization and serves on the governing board of another organization involved in activities similar to those of the employing organization.

What constitutes conflict of interest?

From the above, it is clear that a simple definition of conflict of interest is difficult if not impossible to formulate. It may be possible to arrive at a definition which will avoid all forms of conflict of interest, but such a definition may restrict a person from discharging a calling which one believes to be a requirement of one's faith and values. For example, an individual may take the biblical call to spread the gospel seriously and accept positions on the boards of two or more organizations involved in similar mission activities. Can it be said that such a person is in conflict of interest with both organizations? It would appear that a more fundamental question needs to be addressed in such situations.

Conflict of interest between charitable organizations

Can two or more charitable organizations working in the same activities of service, in response to a call by a higher authority, be considered to be in a conflict of interest with each other? To answer this question, the question of the nature of what constitutes conflict of interest needs to be analyzed a little further.

Conflict of interest arises in situations where a corporation, organization or individual is placed in a position of receiving some form of valuable consideration which is not an integral part of the agreement between the contracting parties. Contractual arrangements by definition require consideration in the form of valuable property, i.e. property, the value of which can be measured against an objective standard.

Charitable organizations exist not for their own benefit nor for the benefit of their members. Rather, they exist to perform one or more charitable activities of benefit to the public at large. As such, it can be said that the owner of charitable property is the public.

If two organizations perform similar activities for the benefit of the public, they cannot be in conflict of interest with each other. The public cannot be in conflict with itself. At best, there can be a discussion about the abilities of each organization to discharge their respective responsibilities. One organization may be more efficient in serving the public than the other, but that cannot be concluded to be a conflict of interest.

It may well be that the more efficient organization is duty bound to share its efficiency capabilities with the less efficient organization. After all, it is the professed commitment of the charity to deliver its benefits to the public which, as noted above, owns both charities. Owners cannot benefit from, or be in conflict with themselves.

Add to the foregoing consideration the concept that in religious organizations certain activities, such as mission work, are done in the public interest because of a faith calling, e.g. the great commission of the New Testament, and there is even less possibility of a conflict of interest arising. All Christian organizations not only serve the same public, but they also serve the same Lord. Therefore, in the charitable sector, and especially in the religious charitable sector, it is not possible for charities to be in conflict of interest with each other

The same argument may not hold true for all not-for-profit organizations. There are not-for-profit organizations, such as boards of trade, which operate for the benefit of the members. In such cases, if the benefits of the members can be distinguished from the benefits of the public, conflicts of interest could arise in relation to such organizations. For example, a golf club is a not-for-profit organization. However, it exists for the benefit of its members. If a board member of the golf club also serves on the board of another competing golf club, that is a conflict of interest.

Conflicts of interest for directors of charitable organizations

If there cannot be conflicts of interest between charitable organizations, the question of conflict of interest for individuals serving on the governing boards of such charities takes on a different character than what would be expected in the for-profit sector. This does not mean that there cannot be conflict of interest situations in which members of the governing boards can find themselves. Such conflicts of interest would be considerations resulting in personal benefits not generally available to the public, instead of benefits accruing to the respective charitable organizations.

Such a distinction both simplifies and complicates conflict of interest issues for the charitable sector. It simplifies issues because it is not necessary to consider conflict of interest questions relating to the relationship between organizations. It complicates conflict of interest issues because such issues often are dealt with by the media and, as a result, by public perception from the perspective of business (profit) activity.

Charitable organizations are not involved in business activities; they are involved in charitable activities. The achievement of profit is the fundamental characteristic of business activity. The profit objective is what makes economic activity a business. Even where there is a commercial or business component to their activities, charities may perform such activities only when they are incidental and/or ancillary to their charitable purposes. The profits from such profit-making activities must be used for the charity's charitable purposes.

This distinguishing characteristic between charitable organizations and businesses results in an intellectual conflict. If the media and public perception reduces all economic activity to business activity, analysis of conflict will always be reduced to the profit motive of either the individual, or the organization. As was noted in the previous paragraph, a charitable organization is active not for the benefit of itself or its members, but only for the benefit of the public. If this fundamental difference is ignored, false dilemmas are created. A false dilemma would be created as a result of the question: "How can one person serve as a director of two charitable organizations involved in compatible missions without conflict of interest arising for either, or both of the organizations?" This is not a valid question.

Conflict of interest or competing interest

The interesting question remains whether certain situations may be referred to as conflict of interest. An example to be considered is when the same individual serves as a member of the governing board of two charities which are both involved in service to the same target group. In this situation, the board member is contacted by a potential donor who wishes to make a large charitable donation for charitable activities which can be performed by both organizations. To which of the two organizations should the board member encourage the donor to make his or her gift? This situation cannot be reduced to a question of conflict of interest. The fundamental element of conflict of interest, i.e. a personal or business benefit, is not present in relation to the board member, or to the two organizations of which he or she is a board member. Neither the board member, nor the two charities, have a potential beneficial interest in the donation. Neither will the board member receive any material or non-material benefit out of the donation. The potential benefit from the donation is vested in the public, no matter which of the two charities receive the donor's gift.

It cannot be denied that potential tension exists for the board member and the charities. The tension between the charities which may be experienced by the board member is not one of conflict of interest, but one of competing interests to serve the public. The board member, in such a case, should leave the decision to the donor. To assist the donor, the board member should disclose as much information as possible about both organizations, pointing out the respective strengths and weaknesses of each of the organizations, and the distinctive approach, if any, of each organization.

The tension that the board member of both organizations faces in the situation described is one of ultimate outcome. If the board member is unable to point out a significant distinctive element, or approach, between the two charities, the board member probably is duty-bound to work towards the amalgamation of the two charities. Duplication without a valuable distinctive element or approach is not in the best interest of the donors or the public.

A conflict of interest can arise in the charitable sector where an individual, or corporation, can receive a benefit which is not available to the public as a whole. From this point of view, all employees of charities are in a conflict of interest situation. The interest of the employee is by definition different from that of the public. The employee seeks to assure himself, or herself, of income security, while the interest of the public is to use as much of the charity's resources for public benefit as possible.

Recognizing that it would not be possible, under currently accepted master servant relationships, to operate charities without employees, it is necessary to develop a conflict of interest definition which takes into account current employment reality.

Conflict of interest defined

For charitable organizations, conflict of interest is a situation where the personal interests of an individual, someone not dealing at arms length with such a person, or a close associate of such person, are in conflict with the best interests of the organization, or the public.

A conflict of interest may occur when:

1. a direct or indirect personal gain, or other valuable consideration is given to, or received by:

   a. an individual, or
   b. a family member or close associate of an individual, or
2. a direct, or indirect advantage, or privilege is given to, or received by:
   a. an individual, or
   b. a family member or close associate of an individual when the individual is in a position to influence the activity which gives rise to the gain or consideration.

The foregoing definition means that all activities which result in a supply or service provided by a charity to an individual, rather than the public at large, results in a potential conflict of interest. The value of such a definition is the recognition that the objectives, or needs, of an individual are not the same as the objectives, or needs, of the public as a whole. Another value of such a definition is to make it clear that all activities of a charitable organization, in so far as they are not applied to the public as a whole, constitute conflict of interest because they are selective activities. No charitable organization can be all things to all people, even where the charity operates completely within its charitable objects.

What can be learned from the above definition is that conflict of interest is not a "dirty" phrase or concept. It recognizes that conflict of interest is a necessary part of every charitable organization's activities. What the definition requires is that mechanisms be created to assure everyone that all individuals are treated equally on the basis of criteria established for all members of the particular segment of the public to which a given activity or benefit may apply. For example, all staff members of the registered charity must be treated equally on the basis of established employment policies and remuneration schedules, and all potential beneficiaries of a charity's services must have access to such services, provided they meet the criteria established by the organization for receiving such services.

Conflict of interest involving members of the governing board

As discussed in earlier chapters, except as allowed by statute or a reference to the courts, a member of the governing board of a charitable organization may neither directly, nor indirectly, benefit from a valuable consideration for goods or services provided to the charitable organization while serving as a member of the governing board. This means that, except with express authority by statute or court reference, no member of the governing board may be paid for any goods or services provided to the charitable organization; whether such a payment be earned as an employee or otherwise. The only exception is the reimbursement of actual out-of-pocket expenses. Anytime that a member of a governing board receives a payment which results in a profit or personal benefit, either directly or indirectly, there is a breach of trust rather than an unresolved conflict of interest. Consequently, it should not be possible for a member of the governing board to receive a direct or indirect material benefit from the charitable organization.

Direct, indirect and perceived non-material conflicts of interests may arise in relation to members of the governing board. For example, a member of the governing board, or those not dealing with such a member at arms length, may be eligible to participate in, and receive benefits of some, or all of the activities of the charitable organization. This example may involve all three levels of conflict of interest.

There is nothing wrong with the member of the governing board, or such member's immediate family members, or close associates, being participants in, or recipients of non-material benefits from the charity so long as such benefits are available to all members of the public on the same terms. For instance, it is a requirement for members of the governing board of a church to be a participant in the primary activities of the church. The primary activities of a church are worship and religious education. Both the individual and his or her family members are beneficiaries of such worship and education activities. In such a case, no one would accuse the member of the church's governing board to be involved in an unresolved conflict of interest situation, either real or perceived.

A conflict of interest can be argued to exist because the participants in worship and religious education constitute a selected few out of the public who could participate in the church's activity. However, such selection is not made by the church, or the members of its governing board. It is a self-imposed restriction by all those who, for whatever reason, choose not to participate in what the church has to offer. The conflict of interest lies in the choice of the charitable activity undertaken in compliance with the church's charitable objects which are not of interest to the majority of the public.

Although it would appear to be relatively clear that the foregoing example involving services primarily of spiritual value does not constitute unresolved conflict of interest, the issue becomes more clouded in the case of charitable activities which involve a transfer of services with commercial value. For example, consider a situation where a relative of a board member of the social service agency receives assistance out of the agency's funds. Even if the criteria for assistance are well publicized and applied in this case, some may hold to a perception that assistance is extended out of favouritism to the board member. This could be the case, especially, if there are not enough funds to serve the needs of all those who are thought by others to be eligible for assistance.

The solution for such conflict of interest issues of board members is not to deny relatives of board members access to the charitable programs of the organization, but rather to see to it, as much as is humanly possible, that all actions are properly documented so that questions of non-material, or perceived, conflict can be answered. It is the obligation of all members of a governing board to resolve conflict of interest issues whenever possible. But to deny members or relatives and associates of board members the right to participate in the charity's activities and services, whether they are primarily of spiritual or commercial value, would be discrimination and contrary to the mandate of the charity.

Conflict of interest involving employees

Since an employee is not prevented by trust law from receiving remuneration, it is possible for an employee to be faced with all types of conflict of interest situations. The two main types of conflict of interest, i.e. material and non-material, are reviewed to determine which types, if any, should be avoided at all costs.

Direct, indirect and perceived material conflicts of interest of employees

An example of an indirect material conflict of interest involving an employee of a charity is: where the charity contracts with a company, the lowest bidder, to provide services. The company is owned by the husband of an employee of the charity, but the officials of the charity have determined that the selected company is competent to perform the service in an efficient and effective manner. Even though the employee might be able to distance herself from the situation by not participating in awarding the contract and by avoiding all opportunities to influence the situation, the husband would still benefit from the contract between his company and the charity. In this case, the possibility of influence by his wife cannot be ignored.

Should a contract between the husband of an employee of the charity be rejected because the husband will derive a direct benefit from earnings because of the contract for services with the charity? Why is the contract with the husband's company any different from the employment contract with the wife? The issue raised here is one not so much of conflict of interest as one of nepotism; the favouritism shown to family members in hiring, or awarding contracts.

In this example, the wife had not participated in the selection process, and the husband's company was competent to perform the required service in a timely fashion. To deny the husband's company the contract solely because he was the husband of an employee of the charity not only would constitute discrimination, but it would also introduce a conflict of interest in relation to the public.

The contract was awarded on the basis of a fair competitive process, and the public, as the charity's beneficiary, has the right to be assured that the resources of the charity will be used in the most efficient and effective manner. Denying the husband's company the contract would result in more resources being used than would be necessary. Such an action on the part of the charity, although applauded by some who have a business view of conflict of interest, might be viewed by others as a breach of trust to the public at large.

Would the situation be any different if there was a direct material conflict of interest between the employee and the charity? What if an employee worked the standard day's hours in an administrative function, and contracted with the charity to clean the office after normal working hours at a cost significantly less than the lowest competitive bid received in an open competition? Whose interests are paramount in such a situation? The interest of those who submitted tenders for profit; the interest of the employee who is looking for some additional income to augment the low wage the charity provides in relation to commercial pay scales for the same type of job; or the interest of the public which is entitled to have the charity's resources applied in the most cost effective manner?

An example of a perceived material conflict of interest is where a charity contracts with a company to provide landscaping services. The landscape company's owner's son is a painter. Can the charity hire the son to provide painting services? An outsider might think the son got the job because he had an "in," since his father already does work for the charity. If the charity hired the son without a formal, documented competitive process, this may be a perceived conflict of interest. To protect the charity from the perceived conflict, the charity would have to hold a formal, documented competitive process to hire a painter.

A charity needs to be as careful about a perceived conflict as it is concerned about real conflicts of interest. While an employee may not be in an actual conflict of interest situation, the public perception that one exists, or may exist, can be equally harmful to the integrity of a charity. For this reason, it is important for every charity to deal with, to guard against, or to resolve perceived conflicts of interest.

Direct, indirect and perceived non-material conflict of interest of employees

Non-material conflicts of interest result when an employee, a close family member, or a friend receives consideration, which cannot be quantified in commercial terms. A direct non-material conflict of interest is one in which the employee receives the benefit directly. For example, as an inducement from a credit card issuer, an employee receives credit card points for charging supply purchases to his or her personal credit card. Assuming that the cost of the supply is the best competitive price, the employee does not receive a material benefit other than that which is available to all credit card holders. However, the benefit is a direct benefit to the employee, because only the employee is able to redeem the points once sufficient points have been accumulated to claim a specific reward. Some have argued that the accumulation of points for using a personal credit card results in a material benefit. However, the organization does not pay more for the supply and the supplier does not collect less for the sale than if the purchase had been made with the organization's cash or cheque. The inducement is offered by a third party unrelated to either the organization or the supplier. Although the points may result in the credit card holder receiving something of value from the credit card issuer when the points are redeemed, that value is not material to the organization, or the supplier.

An indirect non-material conflict of interest could result in the foregoing example if the credit card holder was a family member of the employee rather than the employee herself. The issue remains exactly the same even when the beneficiary of the activity is once removed. Another example of an indirect non-material conflict of interest is where a family member related to an employee of the charity receives public recognition for a gift made to that charity.

As noted earlier, a perceived conflict of interest is the most difficult to deal with, especially when no material benefit results. But since we are dealing with perceptions, the imagination can create conflicts where none exist. Consequently, charities should be very careful not to ignore, but to deal with any perceived conflict of interest situations questioned by anyone, especially when they relate to non-material benefits. An example of a perceived, non-material conflict of interest situation is one where a major donor to a charity asks that the salary of a charity's employee be reviewed. Such a request may be legitimate out of honest concern for the employee's welfare. However, others could conclude that the request is an undue influence on the charity, especially if there is any relationship, be that by blood or friendship, between the donor and the employee.

Developing the policy

In light of the foregoing considerations, every organization should develop a policy to deal with conflict situations. Conflict situations for staff can arise in three primary areas:

1. Employment conflicts, sometimes referred to as nepotism, (the hiring of relatives to fill staff vacancies).

2. Contractual conflicts involving a direct or indirect interest of a staff member in a contract with a supplier of goods or services (e.g. the janitorial services are tendered, and the spouse of a staff member bids on the contract).

3. Territorial conflicts involving conflicts between different departments resulting in protecting one's territory at the expense of the organization's general good.

The board and CEO should see to it that clear policies are developed to deal with each of these types of conflicts. A variety of approaches exist which can be taken in establishing policies in the above three areas. For that reason, rather than recommending specific policies, I will ask questions that need to be addressed in establishing such policies. Some of these questions are:

1. Will the organization allow relatives of current staff members to be employed by the organization?

2. If relatives of current staff members may be employed, will this be done without discrimination as to staff chart level or reporting relationships?

3. If relatives of current staff members may not be employed by the organization, how distant must the relationship be before the organization no longer considers an applicant to be a relative?

4. May the organization enter into contracts for goods and services with persons, businesses, or corporations to which employees of the organization are related by blood or adoption? (Please note that such contracts are not legally permissible in a case where a board member has such a relationship, but that there is no such legal barrier for employees.)

5. If the organization may enter into contracts with parties either directly or indirectly related to employees of the organization, what are the staff member's disclosure requirements.

6. May the staff member who has the conflict of interest, deal with the contract or be involved with its negotiations?

7. Does the organization have a clearly defined tendering policy with dollar minimums for each category of products or services to assure that the best price is obtained?

8. Who should be responsible for developing an interpersonal and interdepartmental conflict resolution policy?

9. Who should administer such a policy, e.g. human resources, senior management? (It should not be the CEO, since care should be taken that an appeal procedure is available.)

Epilogue

In the introduction to this book, we were introduced to John who had been appointed to the board of a relief and development organization. This charity has sizable projects in various countries around the world.

John's understanding was that he could discharge his responsibilities as a board member by making sure that the chief executive officer of the organization discharged his responsibilities properly and that he provided periodic reports to the board. We saw instead that the duties placed on board members exposes them to certain legal liabilities.

The response of those who are asked to serve on the board of a charity should not be one to shy away from such responsibilities. Rather, persons elected or appointed to be board members of charities should familiarize themselves with the duties and responsibilities of directors. In addition, they should see to it that their boards put in place proper policies and monitoring systems so that potential liabilities are substantially reduced.

The attention placed on potential legal liability of board members has caused many good, qualified individuals to question the wisdom of serving on boards of charities. That is an unfortunate conclusion to come to. Although there are standards and duties which board members of charities must meet, they are not onerous, and the potential liabilities can be easily avoided.

The fact that there is greater general awareness about the duties and responsibilities of charity board members should be used by charities to further educate their board members. They should make sure that there is general compliance with the requirements of all specific legislation and the common law obligations. The greater the awareness of common law duties for board members is, the greater is the opportunity to advance the cause of charitable work. By making sure that the charity, on whose board one is asked to serve, is open to an independent review of all of its policies, practices and procedures, both the charity and the new board member stand a better chance of being protected from legal liability.

In the final analysis, it should be remembered that the purpose for serving on the board of a charity is not for personal gain, but to serve in the interest of implementing one or more charitable purposes for the benefit of the public at large. As we saw, there cannot be any personal benefit for serving as a charity board member. A charity board member is entitled to be reimbursed for actual out-of-pocket expenses, but nothing more. Provided, the board member discharges his or her responsibilities as a reasonably prudent person would in the same circumstances, he or she has nothing to fear from trust law.

The courts are also aware of the fact that board members of charities serve as such without remuneration. They will be reluctant to place such volunteers in a position where they would be subject to substantial fines. This consideration should not be cause to become slothful or negligent about ones duties as a charity board member. But, it should be a source of comfort to know that the court likely will be lenient with those who inadvertently are found to be in breach of a specific duty or responsibility.

Likely, the key consideration will always be whether the board members acted in good faith, in the best interest of the charity, and the public, or whether there was an element of self-dealing in their actions. If the latter is the case, the courts will come down as hard on such persons, as it did in the *Toronto Humane Society* case. However, if there was no wilful negligence and self-dealing, the courts will take that fact into account.

One of the best ways to assure that board members have the tools and information available to properly discharge their duties and responsibilities is to provide them with the opportunity for an education program. When new board members are elected, they should be encouraged to attend appropriate training courses and seminars where they are exposed to the materials discussed in this book and other related topics.

Appendix

Evaluation Instrument

To assist board members and boards of charities to determine that they operate in the best interest of the stakeholders and that they are in compliance with the law, I have developed an evaluation instrument. The first section is designed to assist board members to evaluate their own participation and performance. The remaining sections are designed to assist in evaluating the performance of the board as a whole.

The evaluation instrument deals with objective factors, but assigns a weighted value to each item. The weighted value is subjective and somewhat arbitrary. However, each value was assigned on the basis of my assessment of the item's importance to the board member's duties, responsibilities and the effective conduct of a charity's board.

Once each board member has completed the evaluation independently, add the subtotals and total scores of each board member. Divide the result by the maximum achievable score printed immediately below the subtotal or total score. Next, divide by one-hundred to arrive at a percentage. Add the resulting percentages for the subtotals and totals of all the board members. Then divide the resulting totals by the number of board members who submitted evaluations. The final results are the board's and organization's performance percentage in each category as well as the whole.

There is a desire in every evaluation to know the minimum passing percentage. Such a minimum acceptable result is not appropriate in an evaluation instrument of this type. For example, if the organization does certain things which are clearly prohibited by law, an evaluation should fail even if the organization would achieve an overall score of 95%. On the other hand, a result of 50% may not be disastrous for an organization if no specific laws are broken. Having said that, a board should be concerned if the result in any category is less than 75%. The board should also view an overall result of less than 80% as a signal that more work needs to be done in the area of educating and training board members.

The consideration of the first eleven items dealing with a board member's personal performance is different. Each board member can complete an objective performance evaluation based on the scores of these items. If the result is less than 75%, the board member should take immediate action – either to improve the percentage result, or to consider resigning if he or she is satisfied that improvement is not possible.

Charity Evaluation

Board member

Description   Score

1. Percentage of board meetings I attended during the past twelve months (select nearest percentage)

25%	50%	75%	100%
0	1	2	3

   _____

2. Percentage of board committee meetings I attended in past twelve months

25%	50%	75%	100%
0	1	2	3

   _____

3. I received no payment for a supply or service which I provided to the charity in the past year

   true = 5   false = 0

   _____

4. No employee of the charity is my immediate family member (brother, sister, father, mother, son, daughter)

   true = 5   false = 0

   _____

5. Number of consecutive years I have served on the board

   <6 = 1   >6 = 0

   _____

6. My active participation in board discussions is

rare	moderate	frequent
1	2	3

   _____

7. If I abstain from voting I (will) have the reasons recorded in the minutes

   yes = 5   no = 0   _____

8. Unless I abstain with reasons, I participate in every vote coming before the board or committee

   yes = 5   no = 0   _____

9. I have informed myself of the duties of a board member by reading a book or attending a board orientation

   yes = 5   no = 0   _____

10. I participate in all board meetings with independence of mind and am not required to obtain approval for my actions or vote from another party

    yes = 5   no = 0   _____

11. If the situation would arise where I become privy to information which could affect the organization, I will share such information with the full board

    yes = 5   no = 0   _____

12. I will, and where applicable did, report all conflict of interest situations in accordance with the board approved policy

    yes = 5   no = 0   _____

13. I come to board meetings fully prepared; I have read the agenda and all supporting documents

    yes = 5   no = 0   _____

14. I understand and at all times respect the boundaries of the board/staff relationship

    yes = 5   no = 0   _____

Subtotal score   _____

    60

Board quality

15. The maximum number of consecutive years a board member may serve is

2	4	6	8	10	>10
0	1	2	3	4	0

    _____

16. There is a nominating committee to recruit board members (add two points to the score if the committee includes at least a majority who are neither current board members nor staff)

    true = 2 or 4   false = 0   _____

17. The board has adopted a written policy for the nominating committee to recruit new members and/or board members who possess the relationships, qualities and skills appropriate for the organization

    true = 3   false = 0   _____

18. The organization has a membership which is larger than the board

    true = 2   false = 0   _____

19. The number of board members is

<3	3-11	12-15	15-20	>20
0	2	4	2	1

    _____

20. The number of full agenda board meetings per year

          <2   3-4   5-7   8-10   >10

           0   4   3   2   1   _____

21. There is rotation of board members so that a percentage of board members retire each year

         true = 1   false = 0   _____

22. There is a formal education program for new board members either by orientation or a reading program

         true = 2   false = 0   _____

23. The organization has a nominating committee and an audit committee of at least 3 persons (add 2 points if only board members are on the audit committee)

         true = 2 or 4   false = 0   _____

24. The board has each board member evaluate his or her participation at board meetings

         true = 1   false = 0   _____

Subtotal score   _____

                                                29

Board supervision of staff

25. The relationship between board and CEO are clearly documented and followed

         true = 2   false = 0   _____

26. At every board meeting, the CEO is required to submit a written report of the organization's activities since the previous meeting

         true = 3   false = 0   _____

27. At every board meeting, the CEO is required to submit for approval any changes in programs or activities when such proposed changes do not fully comply
with the board's approved policies and previous
approvals

true = 6   false = 0   _____

28. The Board, annually, sets clearly defined objectives
for the CEO and requires the CEO to set such objectives for all staff so that staff performance evaluations
can be measured against such objectives

true = 3   false = 0   _____

29. The board performs at least an annual written evaluation of the CEO

true = 4   false = 0   _____

30 The board has an approved, written hiring and related staff employment and evaluation policy for all
staff

true = 3   false = 0   _____

31. The board has an approved, written conduct policy
for all staff including volunteers

true = 3   false = 0   _____

32. The board requires background checks on all staff
considered for such tasks as counselling and other
one-to-one client or donor services

true = 6   false = 0   _____

33. The board requires its conflict of interest policy to be signed by all staff and volunteers

    true = 4   false = 0   _____

Subtotal score   _____

34

Mission and programs

34. The board has a clearly defined, written value statement which it communicates to all clients, the public, donors, and staff

    true = 2   false = 0   _____

35. The board has clearly defined the organization's plans and has determined that the plans are charitable and within the organization's objects

    true = 4   false = 0   _____

36. The board, at least every five years, reviews its value statement and mission statement and takes action to ensure that strategic planning steps take place within the boundaries of the organization's objects

    true = 4   false = 0   _____

37. The board periodically reviews each program for its effectiveness and service to the public

    true = 3   false = 0   _____

Subtotal score   _____

13

Financial controls

38. The organization annually appoints an external auditor

    true = 3   false = 0   _____

39. The organization makes its financial statements available to the public upon request

    true = 2   false = 0   _____

40. The board periodically inquires from its CEO whether all statutory financial reporting requirements and remittances have been made

    true = 1   false = 0   _____

41. The board approves and monitors the annual operating budget and evaluates the periodic results and the anticipated expenditures for the remainder of the year by means of income and expenditure forecasts

    true = 2   false = 0   _____

Subtotal score   _____

                        8

Fund raising

42. The board has a clearly defined, written fund raising policy

    true = 2   false = 0   _____

43. The board has a clearly defined, written donor designation policy which is communicated in all fund raising appeals

    true = 2   false = 0   _____

44. The organization does not accept donor designated gifts or bequests unless the purpose for which the gift or bequest has been received had prior approval by the board

    true = 2   false = 0   _____

45. The organization never issues receipts for income tax purposes for a payment when part or all of the payment is for goods or services unless specifically authorized by the appropriate taxing authority

    true = 6   false = 0   _____

Subtotal score   _____

                                          12

Board performance

46. There is a written agenda with supporting documents sent to each board member at least 10 days prior to each board meeting

    true = 3   false = 0   _____

47. The meetings are conducted in accordance with written rules of order

    true = 1   false = 0   _____

48. All board committee minutes are sent to all board members and reviewed at the next subsequent board meeting

    true = 1   false = 0   _____

49. Board minutes recording motions and their disposition are approved and signed at the next following meeting and kept in the official records of the organization

    true = 5   false = 0   _____

50. All information necessary for board members to make informed decisions and to make it possible for each board member to discharge his or her legal duties has been shared with all board members without exception

    true = 6   false = 0   _____

51. The board consults professional experts such as lawyers and accountants as appropriate

    true = 5   false = 0   _____

52. The organization does not have alternative, honorary or *ex officio* board members

    true = 3   false = 0   _____

53. The board calls an annual membership meeting

    true = 6   false = 0   _____

Subtotal score

30

Protective instruments

54. The board annually determines that its property and casualty insurance is sufficient and appropriate to protect its assets

    true = 3   false = 0   _____

55. The board has an indemnification policy included in its governing documents

    true = 2   false = 0   _____

56. The board has officers and directors liability insur-
    ance in place

                 true = 2   false = 0   _____

Subtotal score
                                                   _____
                                                     7

TOTAL SCORE
                                                   _____
                                                    193

Index